D1389875

MAKERS
of the
MUSLIM
WORLD

'Uthman ibn 'Affan

TITLES IN THE MAKERS OF THE MUSLIM WORLD SERIES

Series Editors: Professor Khaled El-Rouayheb, Harvard University, and Professor Sabine Schmidtke, Institute for Advanced Study, Princeton

For current information and details of other books in the series, please visit
oneworld-publications.com/makers-of-the-muslim-world

MAKERS
of the
MUSLIM
WORLD

'Uthman ibn 'Affan

Legend or Liability?

HEATHER N. KEANEY

ONEWORLD
ACADEMIC

Oneworld Academic

An imprint of Oneworld Publications

Published by Oneworld Academic in 2021

ISBN 978-1-78607-697-7
eISBN 978-1-78607-698-4

Typeset by Geethik Technologies
Printed and bound in Great Britain by Clays Ltd, Elcograf S.p.A.

Oneworld Publications
10 Bloomsbury Street
London WC1B 3SR
England

MIX
Paper from
responsible sources
FSC® C018072

For my parents, John and Mary

CONTENTS

ACKNOWLEDGMENTS

With my gratitude to:

Asma Afsaruddin, Fred Donner, Tayeb el-Hibri, Aaron Hagler, and Stephen Humphreys for reading and commenting on the manuscript—the input of such a stellar group of scholars significantly improved the final product;

the anonymous reviewer for the helpful feedback, particularly on the first and last chapters;

Jonathan Bentley-Smith at Oneworld for his patience and persistence with this project;

my father, John, for reading the manuscript and confirming that the text is indeed accessible to a non-specialist reader;

my husband, Jim, for the countless pots of tea—he is perhaps the only person happier than I am that this book is now seeing the light of day;

and, finally, to 'Uthman ibn 'Affan, whose life and turbulent times have provided the backbone of my career.

As ever, the responsibility for all errors and inadequacies of this text remains solely my own.

1

CONTEXT

INTRODUCTION

During Ramadan 2001 a Nile TV series, *Heroes of the Faith*, praised 'Uthman ibn 'Affan as an early convert to Islam who became the third caliph (successor to Muhammad), inaugurated the first Islamic navy, greatly expanded the Islamic empire, unified the Qur'an, and then died in 656. These achievements clearly mark 'Uthman as a "maker of the Muslim world." However, they also represent a highly selective remembering of 'Uthman and his impact on the Muslim world. For 'Uthman ibn 'Affan did not simply die in 656, rather he was besieged by fellow Muslims and murdered—an event that sparked *al-fitna al-kubra* (the great trial, schism, civil war). The First Islamic Civil War contributed to the permanent division between Sunni and Shi'i Islam and the establishment of the first hereditary dynasty in Islam. Therefore, in order to understand the Muslim world that 'Uthman made we must address not only the expansion of the Arab empire that took place during his caliphate, but also the crisis that ended his caliphate. The *fitna* inflicted a wound on the collective consciousness of the Muslim community, a wound that is frequently repressed, as it was in the Nile TV series. As a result, the Muslim world has been shaped as much by what it has chosen to forget about 'Uthman as by what it has chosen to remember.

Muslim scholars developed two dominant modes for remembering the early Islamic period. The first focuses on the merits (*manaqib*) or virtues (*fada'il*) of the Companions of the Prophet (*Sahaba*) and subsequent "generations" of Muslims. Works that focus on the virtues of a single individual, group, or generation are generally referred to as *manaqib* or *fada'il* literature; massive compendia of multiple generations or groups are known as "biographical dictionaries." They are all highly hagiographic in nature. A second genre, universal chronicles, focuses on the expansion and development of the Islamic polity from Muhammad's leadership in Medina to the court and conquests of the caliphs. Chronicles are organized by year and focus on military campaigns and reigns. It was during the ninth (third Islamic) century that authors of chronicles and *fada'il* works drew together the circulating reports of what Muhammad and his Companions had said and done to create the foundational narratives of the early Islamic period. Their narratives could not help but be influenced by what had transpired since the seventh century. As a result, the 'Uthman that has shaped the Muslim world is as much a product of the eighth and ninth centuries as the seventh century.

Ninth-century scholars primarily sought to explain what had "gone right" for Islam vis-à-vis other religions and empires, but were forced to address as well what had "gone wrong" in terms of its own internal religious and political divisions. Chroniclers wrote universal histories that placed the rise of Islam as the climax of human history. *Fada'il* works and biographical dictionaries tied this success to the unity and virtue of Muslims, especially the first generation of Muslims. At the same time authors of both genres were engaging in internal debates over who has the right to lead the community and on what basis. Disagreements on this issue began upon Muhammad's death and turned violent during 'Uthman's caliphate. Chroniclers blamed internal social, political, economic, and personal factors on the one hand, and outside forces, marginal figures, and heretics on the other. *Fada'il* works focused on the latter explanations, which were consistent with their portrayal of the unified early Community (*umma*) and the collective virtue of the Companions (*Sahaba*). It was this version of events that came to dominate the narratives and eventually shape the identity of Sunni Muslims.

It was also in the ninth century that differing interpretations about what had happened in the past and what should happen in the present were starting to congeal into what is now known as Sunni and

Shi'i Islam. Although there are different strands within Shi'ism, they all condemn 'Uthman and by extension the other Companions who chose him to be the third caliph. In contrast, and in part in response to Shi'i condemnation, by the tenth century Sunni Muslims were those committed to defending the first four caliphs, including 'Uthman. They refer to Abu Bakr, 'Umar ibn al-Khattab, 'Uthman ibn 'Affan, and 'Ali ibn Abi Talib as the "Rightly Guided" or *Rashidun* Caliphs; their caliphates were portrayed as a religio-political golden age that represented unity and piety, even though 'Uthman and 'Ali's caliphates were scarred by rebellion and civil war. Much of Islamic religio-political theory and rhetoric that has shaped the Muslim world until today emerged directly or indirectly out of responses to 'Uthman's caliphate and the *fitna* that followed.

One cannot understand the Muslim world, past or present, without understanding how Sunni scholars responded to the perceived "problem of 'Uthman" with the two pillars of *umma* and *Sahaba*. The belief in a unified and just community during the era of the Rightly Guided Caliphs, like all origin stories, can be reinterpreted and redeployed again and again. For example, Islamic modernizers in the early twentieth century pointed to 'Uthman's election to the caliphate through a consultative council as historical confirmation of Islam's democratic values. More commonly and persistently, unity of the community and the specter of *fitna* can be used to defend a regime and silence dissent. Alternatively, a government or ruler can be measured against the idealized justice associated with Muhammad and the Companions, judged, and found wanting. The "fear of *fitna*" and the "fight for justice" positions were first articulated in narratives of the confrontations between 'Uthman and his critics, and they have continued to provide rhetorical resonance down to the present.

THE CHALLENGE OF 'UTHMAN

'Uthman was one of the earliest converts to Islam from the leading Umayyad clan in Mecca. The Umayya were among Muhammad's fiercest opponents making 'Uthman's conversion particularly commendable and beneficial to the early community. Furthermore, 'Uthman became the third successor, or caliph, to lead the Islamic Community after Muhammad's death. During 'Uthman's caliphate (644–656) (all dates are references to the Gregorian Calendar, unless otherwise stated), Islam experienced one of its greatest periods of expansion. The Arab forces consolidated control of recently conquered Iraq, Syria, and Egypt and moved beyond these into North Africa, the Iranian Plateau, Central Asia, Armenia, and the Mediterranean Sea. They defeated the Sasanian empire and created the first Islamic navy, captured Mediterranean islands, and engaged the Byzantine fleet off the coast of Anatolia. The Islamic empire of 'Uthman's rule encompassed, more or less, the land that has remained the undisputed heartland of Islam.

However, 'Uthman also presents a major challenge, both then and now. Shi'is claim that when the Companions chose 'Uthman to be caliph they knowingly and willfully rejected the better candidate, Muhammad's cousin and son-in-law, 'Ali ibn Abi Talib, suggesting that they had abandoned true Islam. Sunnis, faced with such charges, were forced to defend the election of 'Uthman as proof of their own orthodoxy and of God's continued guidance of the Community. Furthermore, after years of stunning military victories, by the second half of 'Uthman's reign forces were stalled or defeated on several fronts. It seems very likely that this put a severe strain on 'Uthman's legitimacy as "Commander of the Believers" and may have contributed to the rebellion against his rule. The rapid expansion also severely stretched the embryonic central government in Medina. 'Uthman sought to strengthen the control of the state over administrative and financial affairs as well as the Islamic character of what was on its way to becoming a vast multi-ethnic, multilinguistic, multicultural, and multi-religious empire. 'Uthman required more of the revenue from the conquered provinces to be sent to Medina for the use of the central government. He appointed family members, frequently young men of ability and ambition, whom he could rely on. He also launched a project to produce a single, authoritative codex of the Qur'an. Centralization met with opposition that intensified throughout 'Uthman's caliphate. 'Uthman responded by punishing his critics. Complaints in the provincial centers led to armed bands marching on Medina to compel

'Uthman to either change course, abdicate, or fight. The question lingers until today: was 'Uthman criticized for doing the painful but necessary work of centralization, and thus a martyr for the greater good, or did he bring rebellion and regicide upon himself through his arrogance, corruption, and incompetence?

THE CHALLENGE OF THE SOURCES

It is difficult to exhume the person of 'Uthman buried under the paradigmatic role of a prominent Companion of the Prophet and caliph.

Attempts to reconstruct the history of more than a millennium ago for any region or tradition presents multiple challenges. The sources for early Islamic history and the life of 'Uthman are no exception. First, Muslims initially preserved their history as oral tribal traditions. These have a strong bias towards the behavior of individuals that the tribe wanted to remember and celebrate. As a result, details cluster around particular battles, individuals, acts of heroism or betrayal, but do not collate easily into a single, coherent narrative or address causes and consequences at a meta level. Second, these oral tribal histories were only gathered and written down in histories of the conquests or the caliphate in the late eighth century, that is 150 years after the events they describe. A further complicating factor is that hardly any of these eighth-century histories survive in their original form, but instead come down to us as they were integrated into multi-volume, universal chronicles and biographical dictionaries in the mid to late ninth century. That is 200 or more years after the advent of Islam. By this point the Islamic world was no longer based in an Arabian tribal milieu, but in the medieval metropolis of Baghdad, ruled by its second major dynasty and strongly influenced by Persian and Byzantine intellectual and cultural traditions. Inevitably, historians were tempted to project back anachronistic motivations and levels of centralization. The intervening political and ideological developments shaped how authors perceived and thus told the story of the past. Finally, the ninth-century chronicles sought to place the rise of Islam and the caliphate as the climax of world history. As a result, they are unremittingly triumphalist, especially for the conquests, frequently skipping over setbacks and trials faced by the community and instead portraying a divinely ordained and enabled march towards wealth and dominance.

In addition to the very limited number of sources from the first two centuries of Islam and then a mountain of material from the third, the chronicles and biographical collections do not present a single, smooth narrative of events, but rather keep accounts as isolated reports (*akhbar*) that frequently contradict each other. While maddening for modern scholars, this approach enabled medieval Muslim scholars to legitimize their own points of view by wrapping them in the cloak of earlier authorities. Appreciation and analysis of how chroniclers selected, edited, and arranged their sources has come in recent years to supersede long-standing debates over what, if anything, can be reliably learned about the seventh century from the ninth-century narratives. This biography of 'Uthman reflects a current synthesis (or surrender) in the scholarship as it follows the chapters of 'Uthman's life found in the ninth-century sources, and also highlights the interpretative elements that emerge from close reading of these sources. In this way we get as close to the historical 'Uthman as the sources allow, while also recognizing that what they present is the 'Uthman of the community's collective memory—the Muslim world that made 'Uthman and vice versa.

'UTHMAN'S WORLD

'Uthman lived in a tribal society experiencing rapid transformation in which a new religion and centralizing state catapulted the Arabs into a regional superpower. 'Uthman initially rode the crest of this wave, but was eventually overwhelmed by the tensions between the old order and the new.

Late Antiquity

The Arabian Peninsula and the Arabic-speaking people living there were a part of, rather than cut off from, the world of late antiquity.

We must banish the dominant image of Bedouin on camels emerging out of the desert. While some lived a nomadic or semi-nomadic life, living in towns and settled oases was equally common. Those living in Mesopotamia and in Syria-Palestine were integrated into the social, economic, and political fabric of the two superpowers of late antiquity—the Sasanian Persian empire and the eastern Roman, or Byzantine, empire. Tribes on the edges of these empires were offered titles and stipends in exchange for not raiding local towns and caravans. They also provided much needed manpower as "nomad units" in the exhausted Sasanian and Byzantine armies. Ports along the Persian Gulf and Mokka in Yemen traded with these empires, with Ethiopia, and as far away as India.

Contact with the surrounding empires engendered change. Religion and power went together. Monotheism became a part of the religious landscape. The Himyarite dynasty that controlled Yemen converted to Judaism in the fourth century and was conquered by the Christian rulers of Ethiopia in the early sixth century. Some tribes in Syria-Palestine converted to Christianity. Ascetics set up monasteries in the desert and evangelized local people. In terms of political power, those who acquired titles from the Sasanian or Byzantine empires sought to leverage them into greater influence locally and established short-lived dynasties. Nevertheless, people's primary loyalty continued to be to their tribe.

Tribes

In Arabia in the seventh century (and still to some extent today), people organized themselves genealogically. Members of a tribe were seen as descendants of a common ancestor and took the name of that ancestor, hence the common word for tribe, "*banu*," means "sons of." Large tribes were divided into clans that followed lineage lines and were also referred to as the "sons of," such as the Banu Umayya or the Banu Hashim, Sons of Umayya and Sons of Hashim, within the tribe of Quraysh. Being "family" brought connections and obligations. Solidarity and rivalry were explained in terms of lineage and kinship. However, not unlike the modern nation state, tribes were not as natural or inevitable as they might first appear. While nations invent traditions, tribes invented ancestors. What might seem arcane, inconvenient, or restrictive was in fact very malleable and served a practical purpose to provide protection and cooperation. In other words, a shared distant relative could be "discovered" to facilitate a tribal alliance or merger, or a past slight "remembered" to justify struggles for power or access to limited natural resources. The tribal distinctions were real because they were useful.

There were wide discrepancies in power and wealth between and within tribes. This could be a source of friction and disgruntlement. Caring for vulnerable members of the tribe was a point of honor for the tribal leader, or shaykh. However, not unlike the nobility in Europe, *noblesse oblige* could be more a principle than a practice. Moreover, family fortunes inevitably waxed and waned over time. Once-great "houses" could have honor and aspirations commensurate with a former material wealth that had since been lost. Similarly, previously obscure tribes or clans could rise on the shoulders of opportunity and talent. So, while lineage and family honor were used to explain a tribe's power or prosperity, they were not a substitute for the exigencies of history and the strength of character—as the Prophet Muhammad's life clearly shows.

Muhammad and His Message

Muhammad's career and the Message of Islam challenged the tribal foundations of Arabian society. Muhammad was from the clan of Hashim within the tribe of Quraysh in the city of Mecca. Muhammad's clan was responsible for supplying pilgrims who came to Mecca to visit the *ka'ba* shrine. This was a prestigious role and had at one time been lucrative for the Hashimites. The descendants of Hashim's brother, 'Abd Shams, dominated the regional trade and trade fairs that accompanied Mecca's status as a sanctuary city and juncture on the trade routes in western Arabia. They had become wealthy from this trade, and their influence in Mecca and the region had come to surpass the other Qurayshi clans, including the Hashimites. They were effectively the leaders and stewards of the city. By Muhammad's day the

Banu 'Abd Shams were led by the descendants of 'Abd Shams' grandson, Umayya, and were commonly referred to by that name. Islam intensified the rivalry between the Banu Hashim and the Banu Umayya, what one scholar describes as the "haves" and "nearly hads" of Mecca. Many of Muhammad's earliest converts came from his own clan, like his cousin and son-in-law, 'Ali ibn Abi Talib, or, like Abu Bakr and 'Umar, from other weaker clans within Quraysh. The Umayyads benefitted most from Mecca's status as a trade and pilgrimage center and thus were most threatened by Muhammad and his condemnation of polytheism. One of the leaders of the Umayyad opposition was Abu Sufyan, 'Uthman's own uncle. 'Uthman's membership in the Umayyad clan did not protect him, and he left Mecca along with Muhammad and the other believers in the *Hijra* (emigration) to Medina in 622. In retrospect, this event was seen as so significant that it became the beginning of the Islamic, or *hijri*, calendar. From Medina Muhammad forged a new tribal alliance that slowly surrounded and outnumbered the Qurayshi confederation based in Mecca.

Muhammad was trying to draw monotheists, the faithful or *mu'minun*, of the region together. He presented himself as the heir of the biblical prophets and sought the support of Jews and Christians. The Qur'an clearly condemns Christian doctrines of the incarnation and trinity as polytheistic. But it also praises the piety of Christian monks and distinguishes between righteous and unrighteous Christians. The "constitution of Medina" bound together in mutual support and defense the monotheists of Medina. Being loyal to the Community and accepting Muhammad's leadership, while not necessarily accepting his prophethood or abandoning Jewish beliefs, was enough to be counted among the Faithful.

Muhammad was able to defuse some of the Meccans' objections to his message when he received a revelation that directed him to switch the locus of prayer and devotion from Jerusalem to Mecca. In other words, the *ka 'ba* did not need to be destroyed but purified and restored to a place of worship of the one true God as originally intended by its builder, Abraham, the father of monotheism. Arab identity was being recast as synonymous with monotheism and Islam. Mecca would continue to be a religious and pilgrimage center, but to Allah. Muhammad affirmed this by attempting to make a pilgrimage to Mecca with all his followers in 628. Although his coalition of tribes now surpassed that of the Meccan opposition, he dealt extremely shrewdly with the Qurayshi leadership. He did not force his entry into Mecca, but agreed to return on pilgrimage the following year with the understanding that Mecca would be opened to him and all his followers. A few years later the city surrendered, its inhabitants submitted to Muhammad and became Muslims.

The mass conversion of the Umayyads did not end the rivalry among Qurayshi clans. Whether the Umayyads would be able to use their wealth, networks, and leadership experience to dominate the *umma* as they had the Meccan Quraysh—despite actively fighting against Muhammad until the last possible moment—remained a contentious issue. Muhammad sought to tie the prosperity of individual clans and tribes to the collective success of Islam. He recognized that success required the skills of all Believers. Muhammad appointed some who had opposed him strongly, including Abu Sufyan, to diplomatic missions and military command. Yet Muhammad's inner circle of advisors remained those who had been with him longest. Precedence in conversion (*sabiqa*) was the surest path to prestige and power. This created a new hierarchy with early converts from Mecca on top, followed by Muhammad's "Helpers" (*Ansar*) from Medina, followed by everyone else, including the traditional tribal elite of Mecca. Muhammad and the first and second caliphs, Abu Bakr and 'Umar ibn al-Khattab, had to negotiate the tension between an old hierarchy based on blood and a new hierarchy based on belief. 'Uthman's inability to do likewise was arguably the main failure of his caliphate—a failure that cost him his life.

Caliphate

Our sources use the title caliph to describe 'Uthman during the twelve years he was leader of the new community. In 'Uthman's day, *Amir al-Mu'minin*, Commander of the Faithful, was the preferred title. This should draw our attention to the distance between our ninth-century sources and our seventh-century subject. On Muhammad's death the community fractured along tribal lines as early converts from Medina proposed to break away from the hegemony of early converts from Mecca. 'Umar ibn al-Khattab prevented this when he framed unity not as deference to Quraysh, but to the prestigious early Companion Abu Bakr. At that point Abu Bakr became the first caliph of the Messenger of God, *khalifat rasul allah*. But since caliph can mean both successor, as in the one who comes after, and deputy, the title reveals some uncertainty around what kind of authority the leader should have. For example, there is evidence that 'Umar could have been addressed as *khalifat khalifat rasul allah*, suggesting successor as a chronological marker, but he found this unwieldy and so adopted the title Commander of the Faithful that 'Uthman also used.

The Qur'an says surprisingly little about government or political authority. It was Muhammad's example that made the belief in a single ruler exercising considerable control a religious as well as a political ideal. But Muhammad's authority as a prophet could not be fully replicated. Therefore, the authority of Abu Bakr, 'Umar, and those who came after them had to be worked out over time and in response to circumstances. When the Umayyad caliphs (661–750) adopted the title caliph the connotation was not only of *khalifat rasul allah*, Successor of the Messenger of God, but *khalifat allah*, Deputy of God, claiming authority commensurate with that of Byzantine and Persian emperors. Therefore, ninth-century chroniclers were viewing 'Uthman as a caliph through the lens of a highly evolved office and inevitably projected onto 'Uthman powers that he likely did not have.

Indeed, one of the challenges that faced 'Uthman and the community was the lack of clarity around the authority of the leader. Arabian tribes who had sworn loyalty to Muhammad were not convinced they owed loyalty to Abu Bakr, and he used force of arms to compel them to submit in what became known as the *Ridda* Wars, or Wars of Apostasy. Abandoning the Muslim "tribe" and its head, the caliph, was equated with abandoning Islam itself. While Abu Bakr was successful militarily, questions remained: did political legitimacy require military victory and were Arab tribes submitting to the new "clan" of early converts or to the old tribe of Quraysh? Abu Bakr appointed 'Umar ibn al-Khattab as his successor. On the one hand this suggests he did not anticipate strong opposition to 'Umar and believed his decision would be respected. On the other hand, perhaps he feared the community would fracture if there was not a clear successor.

'Umar was committed to preserving and developing the Islamic identity of the state enshrined in early conversion (sabiqa). To that end he created a registry of all men based on their order of conversion to Islam. Land and booty from the conquests were distributed based on the combined criteria of contribution to the campaign and precedence within Islam: the earlier one joined the larger one's share. Moreover, all 'Umar's advisors were early Meccan converts. 'Umar was also willing to remove leaders with considerable military or administrative abilities for behavior not befitting a Muslim. Ambitious members of Banu Umayya must have wondered how they could improve their prospects in this new order.

The tension between sabiqa and kinship, as the organizing principle of the new state and the basis and limits of caliphal authority, intensified rather than abated during 'Umar's ten-year reign. For what would replace sabiqa when the first generation of converts died—a natural process accelerated by losses due to war and plague? Would it return to pre-Islamic dominance by tribal elites regardless of their commitment to Islam? Or did Islamic leadership mean rule by Muhammad's family or clan as 'Ali and his supporters increasingly argued? 'Umar had ruled largely as a traditional tribal shaykh, but the rapid expansion of Islamic rule during his caliphate meant this basis too was inadequate.

Conquests

During 'Umar ibn al-Khattab's ten-year reign (634–644) Arab armies conquered Egypt, Palestine, Syria, and Iraq. During 'Uthman's twelve-year reign (644–656) they conquered numerous Mediterranean islands and the Iranian plateau and pushed into Central Asia, the Caucasus, and North Africa. In the process they defeated one regional superpower, the Persian Sasanian empire, and seized the eastern Mediterranean territories of another, the Byzantine or eastern Roman empire. Both the reasons for the Conquests and their success remain a topic of fascination and consternation for scholars and laypeople alike.

While we cannot go in depth into this important subject here, it is worth summarizing briefly the situation 'Uthman inherited and our best understandings of it since continuing the Conquests was one of 'Uthman's main policy achievements, even as it stretched his authority and his administration to breaking point.

Scholars agree on a few core reasons for the Conquests, but disagree on how they weigh their relative significance. These are first tribal energies and rivalries directed outward rather than turned on each other. Since Islam functioned as a new super tribe to which Believers owed absolute loyalty they were no longer permitted to attack or raid tribes within the confederation. Likewise, booty, tribute, taxation, and control of lucrative trade routes rewarded the faithful; provided the revenue needed for a society of recently settled nomads; and strengthened the legitimacy of Muhammad and then Abu Bakr, 'Umar, and 'Uthman. It is also likely that members of the new Islamic elite saw an expansion of the state as necessary in order to preserve their hard-won position at the top of the new political hierarchy. More research needs to be done on how economic and environmental changes—which frequently presage conquests and migration—contributed to the Arab conquests.

In addition to the very material benefits of the Conquests, there were ideological motivations as well. Muslims believed that the guidance and leadership provided by Muhammad and then by his Companions, based upon Muhammad's example and the Qur'an, would bring God's ideal just order from which all would benefit. After the *hijra* to Medina, Muhammad had been given permission in Qur'an 22:39 to fight against the Quraysh for their continued opposition to and persecution of Muhammad and his message. The Muslims' victory in battle confirmed God's approval, drew more tribes to participate in the hope of further victory, and by so doing made victory more likely. Many Quranic verses refer to struggling or striving (*jihad*) in the path of God. These can be read as referring first to internal spiritual struggle, second to external but non-violent efforts, such as preaching, and third to violent struggle through fighting and war. These interpretations were and are debated by Quranic scholars. But there are also verses, such as Qur'an 9:29–31, that extol fighting (*qatil*) those who do not believe God and submit. These kinds of verses, combined with militant interpretations of *jihad* verses, provided adequate justification for the initial Conquests. Continued success made the Conquests financially beneficial and a powerful recruiting tool, which encouraged a further strengthening of the religious justification. The historical and legal tradition followed suit so that *jihad*, striving for God, became equated with fighting for God.

It is hard to know whether to speak of Islamic conquests or Arab conquests, or neither. Scholars use both terms, frequently interchangeably, even though they convey two different framings and rationales. Moreover, each term has its own set of problems and limitations. The degree to which a shared Arab identity, based on language and culture, encouraged the peripheral tribes to join the new movement, or the movement's success strengthened a sense of a shared Arab identity remains a matter of scholarly debate. On the one hand there is the view that Muhammad initially saw himself as a prophet for the Arabs, and so there was a drive to unite all the Arabs including those in Syria and Iraq. This put the Arabs on a collision course with the Byzantine and Sasanian empires that controlled these areas. It also meant that, as Arab tribes joined the Muslim Arabs, it left the Sasanian and Byzantine frontiers vulnerable to further penetration. Not all of these tribes converted to Islam, but rather fought alongside the Muslims, apparently making their own calculations as to where their true loyalties lay and how their interests would best be served. This both explains why Muhammad's confederation of tribes attacked Byzantine and Sasanian territories as well as why additional tribes joined them and secured their success.

On the other hand, it is unclear the degree to which there was a shared Arab identity to appeal to. Certainly, at the time of the Conquests the peoples living in the Arabian Peninsula did not refer to themselves, nor were they referred to by outsiders, as Arabs. As mentioned above, primary loyalty was to the tribe or possibly a federation of tribes. Tribes were divided by different ways of life (not all were Bedouin), religion, affiliation with different imperial powers, and even dialects of Arabic. Using the term Arab, therefore, runs the risk of imposing an anachronistic sense of cultural uniformity and ethnic solidarity on the fluid and contested identities of the Arabian Peninsula in late antiquity. As Arabian tribes were drawn into a confederation, first under Muhammad and then the first caliphs, there is a case to be made that it was the shared experience of being conquerors living together in the garrison cities in the provinces that forged, rather than harnessed, a unified Arab identity. The distinctiveness of this identity was then embraced by later Muslim writers and projected back into the pre-Islamic period. Therefore, it can be helpful to use the term Arabian, and Conquests by Arabians, rather than Arab to remind ourselves of what the Conquests achieved not just territorially but also existentially. It also highlights the divisions that continued to threaten the new Muslim community and eventually ended 'Uthman's caliphate.

Describing the Conquests as Muslim or Islamic produces a similar set of problems. Muslims referred to themselves as "Believers" or "Faithful," that is monotheists, and so they may have been trying to unify all monotheists in the region in anticipation of the approaching Final Judgment. This made it possible for Jews, and especially Christians, to fight alongside Muslims. Byzantine and Persian sources refer to the invaders with a variety of terms connoting nomads, desert dwellers, or the descendants of Hagar and Abraham. The descriptor "Islamic" obscures the fact that neither the Muslims themselves nor their opponents viewed the Conquests in the narrowly religious way that the term implies today. It replaces the complexity of the seventh century with the more clearly defined religious identities and divisions found in the ninth-century Arabic sources and contemporary attitudes. In any case, spreading Islam as popularly conceived today does not appear to have been the issue. This may help to explain why mention of conversions, coerced or voluntary, is largely absent from the Conquest accounts. Indeed, in the conquered provinces the Arabian armies created new garrison cities, such as Kufa and Basra in Iraq and Fustat in Egypt, with the apparent intention of keeping themselves separate from the local population. That people were not forced to convert may help to explain the relative speed and success of the Conquests.

Both contemporary Byzantine sources and later Arabic sources speak of death and destruction that accompanies war, but this appears to have been a relatively short window of time before life resumed familiar rhythms. The archeological record does not reflect the razing of cities or evidence of much material destruction. Admittedly, this can be misleading because the early confrontations took place between armies in the field not through besieging cities. Given the armies of the Believers were interested in submission to God's rule and revenue from tribute and taxation, it made little sense to kill those who would pay. Similarly, converts would not pay taxes and instead received a share of the tax revenue, providing another reason why there was little incentive to encourage conversion.

Many cities had paid an annual tribute or tax to Constantinople or Ctesiphon in exchange for the protection and security afforded by the Byzantine or Sasanian empires. When this failed it was hardly surprising that people would pay similar money for similar reasons to the new imperial capital in Medina. Furthermore, the Byzantine and Sasanian empires were ethnically and religiously diverse. The Sasanian state espoused Zoroastrianism, but had Jews, Nestorian Christians, worshippers of Mithra, Arabian polytheists, and others as subjects. The Byzantines had less religious diversity, but at the Council of Chalcedon in 451 the churches of the Middle East split from Constantinople. Consequently, they were often treated as heretics and schismatics by their own Byzantine government. As a result, being treated as a religious minority, even if one was part of the local majority, was not a new experience for the peoples who came under Muslim rule.

The Conquests seem designed to encourage surrender and payment while minimizing death and destruction. This does not mean it was peaceful. Cities and regions resisted strongly. There was destruction and violence, people and property were carted away as war booty and slaves, followed by the imposition of tribute. However, the terms of surrender were more lenient if a city submitted quickly, while fierce resistance was met with total devastation and more punitive payments. This served as a lesson to other communities. It also made good strategic sense if the goal was to take over control at the top with minimal disruption to the flow of goods and harvesting of crops.

In accounting for the success of the Conquests, scholars also point to the internal weakness of the Byzantine and Sasanian empires on the eve of the Arabian Conquests. The Byzantines ruled for centuries the areas around the eastern and southern Mediterranean, including modern Turkey, Syria, Palestine, Egypt, and North Africa. Similarly, the Sasanian, or Persian, empire controlled from Iraq across Iran to Afghanistan. These two regional superpowers had fought each other for centuries; the last great war between them was in the early seventh century. In 602 a military coup left the Byzantine empire weak and divided, and Persian troops conquered Syria, Palestine, Egypt, and Anatolia. The sacking of Jerusalem and the loss of the revenue-rich lands of Egypt were a huge existential and economic blow to the Byzantines and reveal a surprising level of internal fragility. A new Byzantine emperor organized a counter-offensive and quickly retook all the lost territory and marched his own troops to the very heart of the Persian empire, reaching its capital, Ctesiphon, near modern Baghdad. This reversal was possible in part because the Sasanians were also suffering internal political divisions that led to civil war. By the time it ended and Yazdigird III took the throne, Arabian forces had penetrated the western frontier. Moreover, Yazdigird III was very young and untested; the alliances that had undergirded the state remained vulnerable.

At the same time the unification of the Arabian tribes into the new super-tribe of Islam changed the balance of power in the region. Unity under the caliphate meant they were able to put more men in the field, and sustain campaigns through central control and allocation of troops and supplies. They were also led by some very able commanders, whereas the Byzantine and Persian forces were plagued by internal disagreements and divisions. At the Battle of Qadisiyya sometime between 635 and 638, near Ctesiphon, the Arabians won a decisive victory against the Sasanian army and in 636 in northern Jordan they did the same against the Byzantines at the Battle of Yarmuk. Participation in these two battles became a mark of distinction that conferred higher military stipends, a sign of precedence in Islam (*sabiqa*). The loss of the Sasanian capital and the fertile Iraqi lands left the Sasanian state extremely vulnerable. As the Arabian armies marched east in many cases the rulers of local cities surrendered after putting up short and ineffectual resistance. Yazdigird marshalled an army at Nihawand in

642, but he was defeated and the Persian army destroyed, ending the chance of organized military resistance. He spent the following decade traversing the Iranian plateau trying to muster enough support to stop the Arabian advance—without success. Syria and Palestine fell after the Battle of Yarmuk as the Byzantine emperor advised local people not to resist the Arabians, aware as he was that he would not be able to send reinforcements to help them. These communities often lacked their own military force or even weapons. Submitting to the Arabian forces was their best chance to preserve life and property. While the Byzantines were caught up in another succession crisis, the Arabian armies moved on Egypt and made their first incursions into Armenia in eastern Anatolia. The Byzantines, however, unlike the Sasanians, retained their capital, Constantinople, and their lands in eastern Europe and Anatolia which sustained the Byzantine empire for another 800 years.

'Uthman became caliph in 644. He inherited the job of pursuing Yazdigird III and subduing the Iranian plateau. At the same time, he continued to chip away at Byzantine domains and regional dominance. The need for victory in battle to provide legitimacy and lucre was great. But just as important was figuring out how to incorporate conquered lands into the new empire. The booty of war was distributed to those who fought in the campaign minus one-fifth that was sent back to the caliph, as it had been to Muhammad. However, it was not clear how much of the continuing revenue from taxation should go to the fighters who had conquered and settled in the area, or to Arabian tribes who followed and settled after them, or to the central government in Medina. Disagreements over regional autonomy vs centralization in general, and over the allocation of money in particular, became a major source of opposition to 'Uthman's leadership.

THE WORLD 'UTHMAN MADE AND THAT MADE 'UTHMAN

Recognizing that our information about 'Uthman ibn 'Affan comes from eighth-century sources redacted in ninth-century chronicles and biographies, it is imperative that we address a few key intervening developments that shaped the memory of 'Uthman and the concerns of historians and biographers. Of particular note are the first two Islamic civil wars, the rise of two monarchic dynasties, and the division of Islam into two sects, Sunni and Shi'i.

'Uthman's murder triggered the first civil war. 'Ali, Muhammad's son-in-law and cousin, was sworn in as the fourth caliph. From the very beginning he faced opposition, including from key Companions such as Talha, al-Zubayr, and 'A'isha, Muhammad's favorite wife, who had a long-standing grudge against 'Ali. Each side marshalled an army of supporters and they met at the Battle of the Camel in 657. It is so called because the battle raged around the camel upon which 'A'isha rode in an enclosed litter. 'Ali emerged victorious, Talha and al-Zubayr were killed, and 'A'isha sent into retirement. 'Ali was able to consolidate his authority over Iraq and then Egypt, but not Syria. The long-standing governor and commander in Syria, Mu'awiya ibn Abi Sufyan, 'Uthman's kinsman, demanded justice for his murder and did not formally recognize 'Ali's caliphate. This put 'Ali in an impossible situation; his strongest supporters in Kufa were responsible for 'Uthman's murder. 'Ali could not afford to alienate them, never mind punish them. Again, two Muslim armies met, this time in Syria at the Battle of Siffin in 658. It seems that both sides were reluctant to kill fellow Muslims and the situation dragged on in skirmishes rather than full combat until soldiers on Mu'awiya's side put the Qur'an on the tips of their spears and called for the matter to be decided by God rather than strength of arms. 'Ali reluctantly relented; an agreement was signed that they would meet again in a year's time to arbitrate the dispute between them over the punishment of 'Uthman's killers.

The compromise at Siffin greatly undermined 'Ali's authority since it did not acknowledge him as caliph and instead treated him and Mu'awiya as equals. Moreover, in the intervening year Mu'awiya consolidated his position by making deals with influential individuals and tribes while 'Ali struggled to hold his coalition together. In the arbitration, Mu'awiya's representative, 'Amr ibn al-'As, outwitted 'Ali's and the point of debate shifted from punishment of 'Uthman's killers to 'Ali's legitimacy as caliph. 'Ali again withdrew to Kufa, further weakened, until a group of disenchanted former supporters plotted against him and eventually killed him. The murder of the first male convert, cousin and son-in-law of the Prophet, and father of Muhammad's only surviving male grandsons was a further shock to the Community. It marked the end of *al-Fitna al-Kubra*, the Great Schism, the First Islamic Civil War.

By that point there was little opposition to Mu'awiya who became the fifth caliph. He moved the capital of the Islamic empire from Medina to Damascus, indicating the degree to which his authority depended on the strength and loyalty of his own troops and the transformation of the Islamic empire into a regional power that could not be led effectively from Medina in the Arabian desert. Mu'awiya consolidated his authority and relaunched the wars of conquest that had largely halted during the Civil War. He also appointed his son, Yazid, to succeed him. Because he introduced dynastic succession, i.e. kingship like the surrounding un-Islamic governments, there is a permanent stain on his reputation as a Companion and caliph. Yazid killed 'Ali's son, Husayn, and all his family at Karbala in Iraq in 680 when the latter was encouraged to rise up against Yazid's rule in what became the Second Islamic Civil War. Husayn's murder became an unbridgeable breach in the Community from which the characteristics and distinct doctrines of Sunni and Shi'i Islam developed and increasingly diverged.

Shi'i Muslims (from the Arabic "*Shi'at 'Ali*," "faction" or "party" of 'Ali) are those who believe 'Ali ibn Abi Talib and his descendants are the rightful successors to Muhammad as political and religious leaders of the Community. The Shi'is believe that Muhammad appointed 'Ali to be his successor, but disagree in their judgment of the Companions who rejected that appointment and supported the succession of Abu Bakr and 'Umar ibn al-Khattab instead. Today the majority of Shi'is, the Imami or Twelver Shi'is, assert that the first two caliphs were illegitimate and that the Community fell into error when it preferred them over 'Ali. It seems likely, however, that this "rejectionist" position, and its harsh condemnation of the first generation of Believers, evolved over time. In contrast the earliest expression of Shi'ism appears to have accepted the caliphates of Abu Bakr and 'Umar as legitimate, if not ideal. This view is now held by only a small minority of Shi'is, the Zaydis concentrated in Yemen, even though it was the position of 'Ali himself. 'Ali acquiesced to the election of Abu Bakr, 'Umar, and even 'Uthman, reportedly out of a desire to preserve the unity of the Community. This proved futile in the end.

Mu'awiya's Umayyad dynasty ruled from Damascus for almost 100 years. The Umayyads adopted the accoutrements of a royal court and absolute authority like the other superpowers of the region before them, along with accusations of worldliness and abuse of power. Opposition to their rule grew in many quarters, but coalesced around the idea-turned-doctrine that things would go better if leadership of the community resided with someone from among the "people of [Muhammad's] house"—the *ahl al-bayt*. The expectation was that this someone would be a descendant of Muhammad through his daughter Fatima and her husband 'Ali. However, the movement that successfully toppled the Umayyads, the 'Abbasid Revolution of 750, had taken a broad view of *ahl al-bayt* to mean Muhammad's clan, the Hashimites, and the new caliphs were descendants not of Muhammad and 'Ali, but of Muhammad's uncle, al-'Abbas.

The narrower understanding of the *ahl al-bayt* as Muhammad's descendants through 'Ali and Fatima became a rallying point for opposition to 'Abbasid rule, especially when it struggled, as all governments do, to deliver the justice and reform that had prompted the revolution against the Umayyads in the first place. Accordingly, the 'Abbasid government, with its capital in Baghdad, began to suppress and persecute the "Shi'at of 'Ali" just as the Umayyads had done. Like many revolutionaries, once in power, they sought to uphold the status quo. After civil war and revolution achieved little more than one dynasty replacing another, many concluded justice and God's guidance would be mediated to the Community not through Muhammad's blood, but through his behavior. In other words, it comes not through appointing the ideal ruler, but through following all the traditions and practices (*sunna*) of Muhammad and building social and legal institutions based on his example and the consensus of the Community (*jama'a*). These are known as "the People of the Prophet's tradition and community consensus," *ahl al-sunna wa'l-jama'a*, or Sunni for short.

Sunnis and Shi'is use the same Qur'an and have the same view of God and of Muhammad as His Messenger. Their division stems from two irreconcilable versions of early Islamic history. But that difference over time and in the shadow of persecution of the "supporters" of 'Ali by the Umayyad and 'Abbasid state became different understandings, if not of God, then of how He interacts with and guides the community of Believers. Shi'is came to believe that if Muhammad and 'Ali's descendants were given the chance to rule they would "fill the world with justice as it was currently filled with injustice." Shi'is believe that Muhammad appointed 'Ali to be his successor and to complete Islam. 'Ali and his designated descendants, the Imams, had special insight to understand and apply the inner meaning of the Qur'an. While not prophets, these Imams provided a continuation of prophetic power. They were superior men, practically perfect, who like the Prophet embodied and could provide just political leadership and perfect religious guidance. Their presence was a link between the material and the spiritual world. They all lived in hiding and were persecuted and eventually murdered by the Umayyad or 'Abbasid regime. Shi'is disagree on who was the last Imam. A group known as the Isma'ilis who take their name from Isma'il, the son of the sixth Imam, Jafar al-Sadiq, believe in an uninterrupted line of succession down to the present, and follow the Agha Khan as the forty-ninth Imam. The Fatimids who ruled Egypt in the tenth and eleventh centuries and built Cairo were also from this branch of Shi'ism. Meanwhile the Zaydi Shi'is in Yemen take their name from the fourth Imam. However, the vast majority of Shi'is today are "Twelver" or "Imami" Shi'is because they believe the last Imam was the Twelfth Imam who disappeared in the mid-tenth century. Since the Imams had to live in hiding and communicate indirectly and intermittently with their followers, only after an extended period did the followers realize that something had happened to the Imam. But he could not be dead since that would mean the link between heaven and earth had been severed. Accordingly, Twelver Shi'is believe that God preserved his life and hid him away until his return at the Final Judgment.

All of this is anathema to Sunni Muslims. Rather than God's guidance and blessing being transmitted to the Community through

Muhammad's descendants it is done through his Companions and the Community itself. In other words, one becomes an "heir" of the Prophet not through lineage but through learning—those who study, preserve, and adjudicate based on the *sunna* of the Prophet. For Sunnis, approximately 90 percent of Muslims today, defending the Companions as having established the Caliphate and the Community in accordance with God's will is almost as much a point of faith as belief in Muhammad and the Qur'an. To believe otherwise is to suggest the Companions made grave errors and that the whole edifice upon which Islam developed and evolved is faulty. After all, it was these same Companions who preserved and passed down the details of Muhammad's life upon which the *sunna* of Sunni Islam is based. Similarly, to argue that what happened historically was not what should have happened is to suggest that God abandoned the Community—or that the Community abandoned God. Neither view is acceptable. To believe otherwise is to say the Shi'is are correct and to join them in rebellion against the state and society. The virtue of defending communal consensus can give way to the vice of defending the status quo no matter what. The ruler inevitably fell short of delivering an ideal justice, but the office of the caliph became an important symbol of Islamic, or at least Sunni, unity, an unbroken link back to Muhammad and the first generation of Muslims. Moreover, the leadership of the Community became in many ways a collective responsibility in which Islamic scholars and the Islamic law (*shari'a*) they developed, based on the Qur'an and *sunna*, provided the legislative and judicial branch, while the caliph was the executive and the Commander-in-Chief.

Like any religious doctrine the views of the Sunnis and Shi'is were worked out over time and through opposition and antagonism. It is difficult to imagine Sunni and Shi'i Islam without the other; they developed and honed their beliefs in contra-distinction to each other. But as in many religions, it is also a point of faith (if not exactly history) to assert that the fully developed views and practices were strongly understood and held from the very beginning of the movement.

The foundational texts of Islamic history emerged in this context. In ninth-century Baghdad the first biographical dictionaries and universal chronicles were produced. Three sources on 'Uthman from this period are of particular note. Ibn Sa'd (d. 845) was the author/ compiler of the first Islamic biographical dictionary, *The Great Book of Generations*, a multi-volume conservative text that arranges biographies by "generations" of converts to Islam. It provides the template of what will become the accepted biography of 'Uthman. Al-Baladhuri (d. 892) wrote *Descendants of the Nobles*, a massive historical and biographical treatment of the first few generations of Muslims. The third and most important work is a massive history of the world, *The History of the Prophets and Kings* by al-Tabari (d. 923). All three authors relied upon historians of the late eighth century who drew together the circulating mainly orally transmitted accounts and topical histories into single, coherent narratives. The ninth-century authors then cut up and rearranged these sources to fit their own thematic structures. In his treatment of 'Uthman's caliphate, al-Tabari relied heavily on Sayf ibn 'Umar's (d. c.800) history of the first civil war. Sayf's narrative refuted the criticisms leveled against 'Uthman and the Companions recorded in other eighth-century histories. Through al-Tabari, Sayf's narrative entered the historical corpus and often became the preferred version of events; it confirmed the image of the Companions presented in *fada'il* works.

Many of the earlier sources the ninth-century historians relied on were later criticized as "pro-'Ali" by medieval Muslim scholars, and for some time modern Western scholars echoed this assessment. Closer study suggests that they were not pro-'Ali so much as willing to include information that portrayed the Companions in a negative light. Only later, as Sunni and Shi'i identities and rivalries hardened in the tenth and eleventh centuries, were these unacceptable for Sunnis. In part this is because the ninth century also marked the ascendancy of prophetic *hadith*, reports of what Muhammad had said and done, as the basis of Islamic life and law. The primacy of *hadith* required a particular image of the Companions who were the sources of *hadith*. Ibn 'Asakir's (d. 1176) book-length biography of 'Uthman in his multi-volume *History of Damascus* is a good example of this. It appears to be a detailed history, but closer inspection reveals it to be an amplified *fada'il* work. We will see in the next chapter how prophetic *hadith* rather than historical events became the preferred vehicle for commemorating more than remembering 'Uthman.

CONCLUSION

Through the life of 'Uthman ibn 'Affan, Companion and caliph, we catch a glimpse of a critical juncture in the development of the Muslim mission in which the ideals and aspirations of establishing a unified and just community under God's law appear to founder on socio-economic forces and personal failings. Partly as a response to this first great crisis that led to sectarianism and authoritarianism, Sunni Islam developed a deeper existential commitment to the memory of an ideal unified and just community of the pious Companions. We can see this process at work in how the community navigated the challenges to that vision that 'Uthman continued to present.

2

COMPANION

INTRODUCTION

As with other noteworthy figures in Islam, 'Uthman's "character" is understood to mean those actions that constitute his conduct or way of being. This material is most commonly recorded in stand-alone biographies or sections of chronicles identified as *sira* or *sunna*, meaning custom or practices. They are not interested in historical causation, but timeless character traits. Indeed, events regarded as noteworthy are not those that *shape* a person's character, which is understood to be constant, but those that *illustrate* it. A person's life can be seen as a series of photographs selected by face-recognition software rather than home videos documenting change over time. Biography or, more properly, *sira*, present highly idealized individuals as exemplars of eternal virtues. In the case of the Companions of the Prophet, including 'Uthman, these works are hagiographic in nature and bear similarities to sacred biographies in other traditions. They tend to be community-centered rather than author or text centered. The community could be regarded as the collective author as narratives were evaluated based on how they reflected the shared tradition. This meant illustrating the exemplary behavior and ethical dimension that the community expected to be the outcome of the biography. The piety of the individual Companion is proof of the piety of the early Community and vice versa. The sacred memory of the individual and the collective are mutually reinforcing.

Closely related to *sira* is a body of literature known as *fada'il* or *manaqib*, "merits" or "virtues," which were deployed to confer or reflect standing in Islam. This could be applied to groups, such as the Companions, but also to individuals. *Fada'il* works helped to construct the collective identity of the Companions, but they also served to evaluate Companions relative to each other. According to Asma Afsaruddin, virtues, combined with precedence in conversion to Islam, were the criteria for leadership in the early community. Thus, while the content of *fada'il* works may seem primarily pietistic at first, a close reading reveals the ways in which narratives were doing deliberate political work. Leadership based on kinship to, or appointment by, Muhammad only entered the Sunni discourse later to refute Shi'i claims. Closeness to Muhammad, however, was important from the beginning: it was what made a Companion a Companion after all. Moreover, for the Companions, *hadith* provide the bulk of *fada'il* material. Relationship with Muhammad and Muhammad's assessment of the person are of primary importance and provide a powerful political legitimizing tool.

As Sunni scholars turned to the *sunna* of the Prophet to combat the abuses of the Umayyad and 'Abbasid Caliphs and the "heretical" claims of the Shi'is, the reputation of the Companions became even more important. After all they were the source of the growing corpus of *hadith* literature—the reports of what Muhammad had said and done. *Hadith* also became central to determining what was and was not Islamic as Islam spread and engaged different cultures and religions. The lives of Muhammad's Companions became part of the litmus test of Sunni Islam. In the perception of ninth-century Sunni writers they must have been men and women of moral character, their virtue confirmed by their early embrace of Muhammad and his Message. And the Community that they and Muhammad established first in Medina and then in western Arabia also must have been distinctive for its virtue, justice, and unity. Otherwise what good, or how true, could Islam be?

The forces pushing for a highly idealized image of the Companions were furthered by a Quranic moral sensibility that stresses the idea of fixed characters who are either righteous or wicked. People do not become one or the other, rather their actions and choices reveal their core nature as being one or the other. For example, the second caliph, 'Umar ibn al-Khattab, had what could be described as a radical conversion experience. He had been a fierce opponent of Islam to the point of taking up a sword with the intent of killing Muhammad and of beating his own sister for reciting a Quranic passage. Upon hearing the passage, however, 'Umar was convicted, sought out Muhammad and embraced Islam. Despite this transformation what is frequently highlighted in *fada'il* works is that his virtues of honor and conviction remained constant. Whereas before they had worked against him leading to arrogance, after he became a Muslim his good qualities fully developed and benefitted all. In any case, the direction of 'Umar's development was towards greater goodness, whereas 'Uthman appeared to regress. 'Uthman had to be a "good person" since he was an early convert to Islam and trusted Companion of the Prophet. And yet his caliphate went horribly wrong and serious charges were leveled against him. The tradition has come up with four ways of dealing with this. One is to point to symbolic and portentous events halfway through 'Uthman's caliphate when he "changed," or rather the tide turned against him. Second, the events of 'Uthman's caliphate were an anticipated (prophesied) test of the community. Third is to promote narratives that blame everything on a few marginal conspirators who not only plotted to destroy 'Uthman, but Islam itself. Fourth is to be silent about the accusations against 'Uthman while he was caliph and be very loud about the praiseworthy things he did while Muhammad was alive, that is, as a Companion of the Prophet. While the first three are adopted to varying degrees in chronicles, this final approach is the one used by the authors of *fada'il* literature.

Over time *fada'il* had a profound impact on portrayals of 'Uthman's character in all sources. First is 'Uthman's early conversion. This is noteworthy because to convert when Muhammad was still facing resistance in Mecca, as 'Uthman did, is to show a level of dedication and shared experience of persecution in contrast to those who converted after the tide had turned in Muhammad's favor. Second is a particular virtue or character trait that benefits the community. In 'Uthman's case it is his generosity in the form of financial support to Muhammad and the community at three strategic points.

Third is 'Uthman's relationship with Muhammad vis-à-vis the other three Rightly Guided Caliphs that supports the order of the first four caliphs. Fourth is that Muhammad reportedly foretold that 'Uthman would die a martyr. 'Uthman's financial support for Muhammad and the early community, and reports that Muhammad promised him a place in Paradise as a result, is an eternal vindication that counters accusations of abuse while 'Uthman was caliph. Similarly, 'Uthman's status as a martyr offers a final verdict in favor of 'Uthman and against his attackers and killers. As a result, treatment of 'Uthman's character in *fada'il* works and elsewhere say virtually nothing concrete about 'Uthman's caliphate and yet the events of 'Uthman's caliphate are ever present, just off stage, in portrayals of his character. What the tradition chose to prioritize about 'Uthman's conduct as one of Muhammad's Companions was intended to act as a vindication of the Community that chose him to be the third caliph and of 'Uthman's behavior while caliph. As the category "Companion of the Prophet" became more robust in Sunni self-understanding, aspects of 'Uthman the individual and 'Uthman the caliph were regarded to be superfluous or subversive and filtered out.

THE MAN

References to 'Uthman's appearance are found in some early biographies with a few summary remarks appearing in most chronicles and *fada'il*. Al-Baladhuri (d. 892) provides one of the most complete descriptions of 'Uthman's appearance and family life. 'Uthman was of average stature, "not tall and not short;" his face was handsome; he was delicate-skinned, dark-colored, thickly bearded, big-boned, broad-shouldered, densely-haired, and he used to dye his beard. He plaited his hair in locks and strengthened his teeth with gold. His clothing also merited comment, as accounts mention the color and quality of his cloaks. While 'Uthman may not turn heads today, according to al-Mada'ini, when the Prophet sent something to 'Uthman with a female messenger, she was late in leaving 'Uthman's house and when she did finally return the Prophet said: "I see you must have remained looking at 'Uthman and Ruqayya ['Uthman's wife and Muhammad's daughter] trying to decide who is better looking."

In early sources one finds reports that portray 'Uthman as a sensitive family man or a passionate or frail older man. 'Uthman was reported to hold each newborn son near to him and smell him. When asked why he did this, he explained that it was so his heart would be "touched with love and tenderness" for the child if anything should happen to it. Purportedly, 'Uthman performed the purifying ablutions before each prayer because he was incontinent. Or consider this report of 'Uthman's wedding night to Na'ila bint al-Farafisa:

> When she came to 'Uthman, he sat on a couch and she was seated on a couch. Then he removed his headdress and his baldness was apparent. He said to her: 'do not hate what you see of my baldness, for behind it are things you will like.' So she said: 'I come from women who consider their best husband the shaykh who is a sayyid.' He said: 'Either you come to me or I come to you.' She said: 'I have not undertaken any distance greater than the width of this house [i.e. she is not tired in spite of her journey].' Then she rose and sat next to him and he caressed her head and prayed for her. Then he said: 'remove your wrap.' So she removed it. Then he said: 'remove your veil.' So she removed it. Then he said; 'remove your dress.' So she removed it. Then he said remove your undergarment [loincloth].' She replied: 'that is your job.' And she remained in his house until he was killed. (Al-Baladhuri, *Ansab al-Ashraf*, 496)

This very human and intimate portrayal is gradually supplanted in the literature by a focus on 'Uthman's marriage to two of Muhammad's daughters—something that is largely ignored in early histories and biographies.

Early sources also provide snippets of 'Uthman's personal habits or virtues that will eventually be overshadowed by the paradigmatic narrative developed in *fada'il* works. Occasionally sources will mention that 'Uthman did not let a day go by without reciting the Qur'an; he prayed and fasted regularly and was known to sleep in the mosque. He was observed in the mosque asking people about their journeys, their news, and their sick. He was knowledgeable, truthful, and modest. In contrast, what receives more attention, and the tradition treats as a defining aspect of 'Uthman's character, was that he was among the first converts to Islam. This is praiseworthy because he not only perceived the truth of Muhammad's message, but was willing to face persecution for that truth. Early converts provided support and encouragement; they strengthened the community simply by their presence. More significantly, early conversion was used to compare the competing merits, and right to leadership, of different Companions.

PRECEDENCE IN ISLAM (*SABIQA*)

'Uthman was one of the earliest converts to Islam. According to Ibn Ishaq, 'Uthman was among a group of men that Abu Bakr, shortly after his own conversion, brought to Muhammad and who then accepted Islam as well. 'Uthman's conversion, recorded by Ibn Sa'd (d. 845), was not only early, but miraculous. 'Uthman was awoken from sleep by a voice telling him a prophet had arisen in Mecca and so 'Uthman sought out Muhammad, listened to him recite the Qur'an, and accepted Islam. This account argues that God chose 'Uthman before 'Uthman chose God.

A key part of the merit bestowed on early converts was due to the persecution they experienced for the sake of Islam. 'Uthman's conversion was public and he was pressured by his uncle to give up this new religion, but refused to do so. "His uncle al-Hakam b. Abu'l-As tied him up firmly and he said: 'do you give up the faith of your fathers for a new faith? By God, I shall never untie you!' but when he saw that he was unyielding in his religion, he left him alone" (Al-Baladhuri, *Ansab al-ashraf*, 482). Furthermore, 'Uthman's mother refused to eat any of the food or drink he provided for the family until he recanted. She moved out of his house, but after a year she gave up and returned home. Even so, these accounts of 'Uthman's personal experience of persecution are less prominent in the literature than 'Uthman's participation in the communal experience of flight from persecution.

By the fifth year of Muhammad's preaching in Mecca, the fledgling Muslim community was so vulnerable that the decision was made for many of them, including 'Uthman and Ruqayya, to emigrate to Abyssinia where they found protection under the Christian emperor there. This became known as the first *hijra*. A few years later, in 622, most of the Muslims from Mecca and Abyssinia emigrated to Medina. The ability to establish publicly and openly a Muslim community there was seen as so significant that the *hijra* to Medina became the beginning of the Islamic calendar. To have participated in both *hijras*, as 'Uthman did, was a sign of early commitment, when the costs were high, and thus a mark of prestige. It is this act that generally serves as "exhibit A" in praise of 'Uthman. *Fada'il* works either begin with multiple references to it or juxtapose it with complaints against 'Uthman's actions while caliph, for which it serves as mitigating evidence.

Another key marker of prestige and precedence in the early community was participation in the Battle of Badr (624), the Battle of Uhud (625), and the "Oath of Satisfaction (*Ridwan*)" (628). And yet 'Uthman was not present for any of these. The first took place when a group of Muhammad's followers attacked a Qurayshi caravan at a place called Badr. Despite Muhammad's forces being outnumbered, they triumphed and seized a great deal of booty. This victory over the Quraysh of Mecca was a big boost to Muhammad and his followers in Medina. To have participated in this battle became what distinguished the "first generation" of Muslims from subsequent generations. 'Uthman did not take part in the raid at Badr because he was tending to his ill wife, Ruqayya, on what would turn out to be her deathbed. Accordingly, Muhammad gave 'Uthman a share of the booty marking him as an honorary "participant of Badr."

The following year the Meccans attacked Medina in the Battle of Uhud. The Meccans triumphed on the field, but Muhammad and his followers held on to the city. 'Uthman fled from the fighting and there are no known mitigating circumstances. Mention of 'Uthman's flight does not appear in key early sources, but criticisms of 'Uthman must have been circulating because ninth-century authors of *fada'il* literature make a point of declaring that Muhammad forgave 'Uthman for Uhud.

The Oath of Satisfaction in 628 was another significant milestone in the life of the early community. Muhammad and his followers were now the dominant power in the region; they marched on Mecca intending to enter the city as pilgrims. Muhammad had sent

'Uthman ahead to negotiate, but word came back to Muhammad that 'Uthman had been captured and killed. As the pilgrimage was on the verge of being transformed into a raid, Muhammad's followers reaffirmed their loyalty and commitment to fight and die for him in "the Oath of *Ridwan*." Before things could go any further, however, the news reached Muhammad that 'Uthman was not dead. Muhammad then negotiated a compromise with the leaders of Mecca, the Treaty of Hudaybiyya, regarded by the tradition as a diplomatic triumph. Muhammad's return to Medina on the guarantee that the following year he and all his followers could enter Mecca unopposed was effectively a Meccan surrender. Those seeking to malign 'Uthman point out that he was not present at the Oath of Satisfaction. Authors of *fada'il* works point out that 'Uthman's absence was due to the honor of being chosen as an ambassador by Muhammad; they also assert that Muhammad subsequently exchanged a personal pledge of loyalty with 'Uthman.

In Sunni chronicles these events are relayed without additional commentary among the events of their respective years, but 'Uthman's absences while a Companion of the Prophet were drawn into debates over 'Uthman's legitimacy as caliph. Early *fada'il* works contain reports in which someone objects to 'Uthman on the grounds of his absences and then someone else explains the circumstances that exonerate 'Uthman in the case of Uhud and elevate him in the case of Badr and *Ridwan*. Later *fada'il* works mention Muhammad's special provision for 'Uthman after Badr and after *Ridwan* without the corresponding accusations of absence. As a result, 'Uthman's close relationship with Muhammad is the enduring legacy and the traces of controversy gradually disappear from the Sunni narratives.

GENEROSITY

In early *sira* sources 'Uthman's wealth and generosity are treated in ambivalent terms, but over time *fada'il* works cultivate them into a formulaic virtue aimed at diffusing accusations of financial abuse and nepotism leveled against 'Uthman during his caliphate. Initially portrayals of 'Uthman's wealth convey a general liberality. Descriptions of 'Uthman's appearance clearly mark him out as a wealthy person with numerous references to his dyed and expensive clothing, including on occasion the cost of a particular item. For example, 'Uthman is described wearing a fine woolen cloak that he said he wore to please his wife. Or, when he met a young boy in the mosque, he gave him 1000 dinars. 'Uthman also provided food for Muhammad and his wives as well as for others he learned were in need. At the same time 'Uthman spent lavishly on his family. As to the source of 'Uthman's wealth, we are told he "trafficked in goods and kept half of the proceeds."

These reports sit uneasily with those that describe 'Uthman abusing the public treasury once he became caliph. Ibn Sa'd, compiler of the oldest extant biography of 'Uthman, concludes his brief section on 'Uthman's caliphate with the observation that 'Uthman favored Quraysh, gave his cousin Marwan a fifth of the booty from the conquest of North Africa, gave to his family from out of the public treasury, and that the people started to detest him for this. 'Uthman's recorded response: "Abu Bakr and 'Umar interpreted that this money was forbidden to themselves and their kin; I have interpreted it as appropriate to my kin." Al-Baladhuri's biography of 'Uthman includes the section: "mention of what they have denied of the *sira* of 'Uthman b. 'Affan and his affair" which presents a litany of accusations against 'Uthman, many of which revolve around 'Uthman's misuse of money during his caliphate. Accounts of how much 'Uthman spent on members of his family continued to circulate in Islamic chronicles. According to some accounts 'Uthman gave the fifth of the booty from the conquest of North Africa to Marwan as a dowry when 'Uthman married his daughter to him. Similarly, when 'Uthman married off another daughter he ordered the governor of Basra to pay the dowry of 60,000 dirhams from the treasury there. Or they point out the amount of wealth and size of the houses of 'Uthman and his companions and contrast this negatively with the simple life style of 'Uthman's predecessor, 'Umar ibn al-Khattab.

What are we to make of these accusations? Do they reflect 'Uthman's greed or his liberality? Alternatively, do they reveal little about 'Uthman's personality and more about a moment when the ruler's relationship with the treasury was changing? It is impossible to answer these questions definitively because the sources are caught up in the Sunni–Shiʻi rivalry generally, and the 'Uthman controversy specifically. Early descriptions of 'Uthman's wealth and generosity during Muhammad's lifetime can be read as refuting accusations of abuse once 'Uthman became caliph. Surely a wealthy man like 'Uthman had no need to dip into the public treasury. From the range of generous acts that appear in early *sira* material, the *fada'il* sources focus on three paradigmatic acts of financial support that 'Uthman gave to the early community and for which Muhammad promised him a place in Paradise. They indirectly refute specific accounts of later financial abuse, and at the same time Muhammad himself issues the ultimate verdict on 'Uthman's life and caliphate.

As with the three absences, the three "purchases" appear in early histories within the chronological flow of events and without fanfare. These are 'Uthman buying the well of Ruma in Medina for the Muslims' use; equipping the "army of al-'Usra" for the raid on Tabuk in the year 630; and purchasing land next to the mosque in Medina in order to enlarge it in 649. In the *Life of Muhammad* it is noted that, in preparation for the expedition against Tabuk, Muhammad urged and persuaded the people of means to help in meeting the expenses and to provide mounts, thereby storing up reward with God. 'Uthman ibn 'Affan spent a huge sum, more than anyone had ever done, on this expedition. In relation to land for the mosque, the chronicles record that 'Uthman sought to enlarge the mosque by purchasing the adjoining land, but the people on the land refused to sell. 'Uthman tore down their houses and expanded the mosque anyway even as the people shouted in protest. Although 'Uthman compensated them financially, this receives less attention in the sources. Instead it acts as an example of growing resentment against 'Uthman. This makes sense since the chroniclers are at this point seeking to explain the crisis that was soon to befall 'Uthman, his caliphate, and the entire community.

In contrast to these histories, Muhammad's praise for 'Uthman's three acts of financial support comes to dominate the entire narrative in some *fada'il* works. "The Prophet said: 'he who digs the well of Ruma will have Paradise.' 'Uthman dug it. He also said: 'he who equips the army of al-'Usra [i.e. for the raid of Tabuk] will have Paradise.' 'Uthman equipped it." Rather than the purchase of land to widen the Medina mosque during 'Uthman's caliphate, *fada'il* works focus on 'Uthman's contribution to the mosque while Muhammad's Companion. A frequently cited *hadith* has Muhammad promising a home in Paradise to 'Uthman for building God a home on earth. In similar *hadith* Muhammad states that after 'Uthman has expended money for the community he will not need to do anything more. In other words, his place in Paradise is assured. This clearly illustrates how *hadith* and 'Uthman's contribution to the early community could act as a verdict on 'Uthman's life. As the *fada'il* genre developed, these *hadith* were frequently incorporated into later chronicles, framing or replacing controversial aspects of 'Uthman's caliphate.

In many chronicles the significance of 'Uthman's strategic purchases is incorporated into the narrative of 'Uthman's caliphate at the climax of the rebellion against him. Rebels had besieged 'Uthman in his house and as the siege dragged on they eventually prevented 'Uthman from participating in prayers at the mosque and, by some accounts, prevented water from being taken in to those inside the house. At that point 'Uthman confronted them pointing out that they were preventing him from praying in a mosque when he had spent money to enlarge the mosque, and they were preventing him from drinking water from the very well he had purchased for the Muslims. For those familiar with *hadith* this would no doubt draw their attention to 'Uthman's status as a Companion and his promised place in Paradise without breaking with the narrative flow of events.

It is thanks to *fada'il* works that the *hadith* about the well, the army, and the land became absolutely constitutive of the memory of 'Uthman and one of the reasons for his inclusion in the "Ten Promised Paradise." The Ten Promised Paradise refers to ten Companions whose actions elicited from Muhammad the promise of a place in Paradise. While reference to the chosen ten appears in ninth-century sources, it did not receive much attention until the eleventh century; from the twelfth century onwards, entire books were devoted to the *fada'il* of the Ten Promised Paradise. According to Maya Yazigi the timing, the number, and that all ten were from the tribe of Quraysh, suggests that this category gained traction as a part of Sunni propaganda aimed at "strengthening Sunni communal identity." It contrasted the ten Companions with the twelve Shi'i Imams and reaffirmed the legitimacy of the first three caliphs against Shi'i claims. The conclusion that the community chose the right person to be the third caliph when they chose 'Uthman, and that he was not responsible for the *fitna* that ended his caliphate, rested in part upon 'Uthman's three praiseworthy purchases and Muhammad's guarantee that he would be in Paradise with other key Companions.

MUHAMMAD AND THE *RASHIDUN* CALIPHS

While 'Uthman no doubt had numerous and varied interactions with Muhammad, those that have crafted the collective memory of 'Uthman focus on his relationship with Muhammad in comparison with the other *Rashidun* caliphs. During the battle at Badr, Ruqayya, Muhammad's daughter and 'Uthman's wife died. Muhammad decided to have another daughter, Umm Kulthum, marry 'Uthman. Most early sources either mention this in passing or not at all. However, over time we see in the sources a marshaling of *hadith* that highlight its significance. Muhammad states that God sent the angel Gabriel to tell him to marry Umm Kulthum to 'Uthman. Muhammad states that he would marry a third daughter to 'Uthman if he had one, and in some versions, up to forty daughters. Some sources point out that 'Uthman was the first man in history to marry two daughters of a prophet. This would earn 'Uthman the title by which he is known until today, "*Dhu al-Nurayn*," the possessor of the two lights. Marriage to two of Muhammad's daughters clearly cuts across Shi'i claims based on 'Ali's kinship with Muhammad and marriage to Muhammad's daughter, Fatima. In ways similar to the treatment of 'Uthman's wealth and support for the community, treatment of 'Uthman's marriages reflects the development of the Sunni response to the Shi'i claim to leadership based on kinship with Muhammad. 'Uthman's identity as one of the Ten Promised Paradise and the *Dhu al-Nurayn* grew in significance over time.

There is another thematic cluster of *hadith* that appears in early *hadith* collections and consistently dominates *sira* and *fada'il* of 'Uthman. It defends the order of the first caliphs and 'Uthman's behavior during the *fitna*. It is guaranteed to appear in the shortest of *fada'il* works and make up a considerable portion of longer works through repetition in all its variant versions and chains of transmission. In this *hadith* Muhammad is described reclining in his room or sitting at a well; the future caliphs, Abu Bakr, 'Umar, and then 'Uthman each request and are granted permission to join him. Muhammad does not adjust or close his robes for Abu Bakr or 'Umar, but he does do so when 'Uthman enters. After they leave, 'A'isha asks him why he didn't close his robes for her father, Abu Bakr, or for 'Umar, but did close them for 'Uthman. Muhammad responds: "Should I not show respect to one to whom even the angels show respect?" Moreover, in some versions, when Muhammad grants permission for Abu Bakr and 'Umar to enter he says: "admit him and give him the glad tidings of entering Paradise." However, in the case of 'Uthman, he hesitates and then says: "admit him and give him the glad tidings of entering Paradise with a calamity that will befall him!"

This remarkable *hadith* elegantly and efficiently places the first three caliphs in the order of their caliphates, while at the same time ignoring 'Ali and highlighting 'Uthman's personal piety and close relationship with the Prophet. Even more importantly, it presents the first *fitna* as something foreseen by Muhammad, defending 'Uthman as he remains one of those promised Paradise. In variations of this *hadith* Muhammad makes 'Uthman promise not to "remove the shirt of authority" that will be placed upon him nor to resist his fate. These statements further exonerate 'Uthman, explaining why he did not step down from power when opposition to him grew and why he did not defend himself against his besiegers and murderers. The import of this *hadith* is bolstered by others that frequently appear in works on 'Uthman's merits and virtues, namely that he died a martyr. Muhammad reportedly referred to Abu Bakr, 'Umar, and 'Uthman as "the friend and the two martyrs." By foretelling the *fitna* and 'Uthman's death, Muhammad declares 'Uthman and the Companions innocent. One cannot help but regard *hadith* like this to be a *post facto* response to the crisis that befell the community during 'Uthman's caliphate.

These *hadith* eventually get included in chronicles covering 'Uthman's caliphate and so act as a final framing or vindication of 'Uthman. For example, al-Baladhuri, whose biography of 'Uthman is primarily a comprehensive catalog of 'Uthman's failings as a caliph, includes accounts of 'Uthman's murder in reports that portray 'Uthman as a martyr who willingly sacrificed himself out of obedience to the Prophet and in what turned out to be a fruitless effort to prevent internal divisions and bloodshed. And in his history of the world, the great fourteenth-century chronicler Ibn Kathir includes a section on "some of the reported hadith in the *fada'il* of 'Uthman" in his coverage of 'Uthman's caliphate. Namely all the things presented in this chapter. *Hadith* that promote 'Uthman's virtues and merits as a Companion promulgated in the *fada'il* literature, and designed to foster popular piety, have been far more significant than the historical record of 'Uthman's caliphate in shaping Muslim collective memory of 'Uthman.

CONCLUSION

'Uthman ibn 'Affan was an early convert, a close Companion of the Prophet, and the third caliph. However, his caliphate was marred by controversies that culminated in rebellion and regicide. Nevertheless, 'Uthman's early conversion and Muhammad's praise of 'Uthman for his financial contribution to the community come to loom large in the *sira* material. These are clearly designed to act as defenses of 'Uthman becoming caliph and of his behavior while caliph. Treatment of 'Uthman's merits and virtues illustrates three aspects of Islamic history and historiography regarding the Companions of the Prophet. First, the character of the individual serves primarily as an illustration of the virtue of the collective. This leads to the second, namely, that pietistic acts during Muhammad's lifetime, preserved in *hadith*, and propagated in *fada'il* works, provide the interpretive lens for political policies later. Third, the first two developed in the context of debates over who should lead the community and on what basis. These in turn were drawn into Sunni–Shi'i polemics, making criticism of the

Companions an existential threat to Sunni Muslims. Accordingly, the Sunni establishment crafted a *sira* of 'Uthman that was consistent with the image of the Companions that was needed to refute Shi'i claims on the one hand and defend *hadith* as a foundation of Islam on the other. A similar process of validation and vindication was at work in the narration of 'Uthman's election to the caliphate.

3

CONSULTATION

INTRODUCTION

In 644 'Umar ibn al-Khattab, the second caliph, was fatally stabbed by a Persian slave; as 'Umar lay dying he commissioned six Companions of the Prophet to form a consultative (*shura*) council and choose one of their number to be the next caliph. They chose 'Uthman ibn 'Affan. While the principle of *shura* had precedents in Arabian tribal society, 'Umar made provisions that formalized the process in innovative ways. The intent however was the same: to achieve consensus around a new leader when there were multiple viable candidates and no clear successor. That there was no agreed upon successor is the key to the story. How and why was 'Uthman chosen? More importantly, why was he chosen over 'Ali ibn Abi Talib? How genuine or robust was his support? How could he have been the right man for the job in light of how his caliphate ended? The answer to all of these questions is contested in the sources. In fact, in the *shura* "the problem of 'Uthman" threatens to become a "problem of the Companions" for they were the ones who elected him. As the preservers and transmitters of Muhammad's legacy, much of Sunni Islam depends upon their character and reputation. As a result, the stakes are very high indeed.

Our earliest extant sources from the ninth century combine different accounts from the eighth century so that there is no single, smooth narrative of events. The variations found in ninth-century chronicles however, are primarily over details, while there is broad consensus that the *shura* was marred by personal ambition and communal division. They suggest that the outcome was tilted in 'Uthman's favor by his family connections and that 'Ali ibn Abi Talib only gave 'Uthman the oath of loyalty (*bay'a*) under duress. Despite being critical of 'Uthman and the Companions, these narratives are trying to defend 'Umar, the process of the *shura*, and its outcome. They are also using the *shura* to engage ongoing debates about the basis of caliphal authority generally and the 'Abbasids specifically. On two points the earliest accounts of the *shura* uphold Sunni orthodoxy: they argue the caliphs are subject to the Qur'an and the *sunna*, and the 'Abbasids, not the descendants of 'Ali, are the rightful rulers. Nevertheless, since the Companions are maligned these accounts are denounced as "pro-'Ali" by later writers. Authors of *fada'il* and polemical works, and some chroniclers, greatly censor the *shura* accounts to produce an abbreviated narrative that portrays the Companions as quickly and unanimously choosing 'Uthman—"the best of those [Companions] who remained [alive]." This is not surprising. Shi'i Muslims came to regard the *shura* as a notorious moment of betrayal and perfidy when the Companions rejected Muhammad's desired successor, his nephew and son-in-law 'Ali ibn Abi Talib, in favor of 'Uthman ibn 'Affan. Thus, anything that portrays the *shura* proceedings as contentious or suggests that 'Uthman was not the only choice could be accused of Shi'ism by association. Therefore, the significance of the *shura* for 'Uthman's own life is overshadowed by its significance for the life of the entire Islamic Community.

Because the sources are written long after the fact and clearly doing significant ideological work, can we learn anything from them about how 'Uthman became the third caliph? Certainly, we need to be cautious. It is possible that what has come down to us is a pro-'Ali polemic against the Companions edited and overlaid with pro-'Abbasid apologetic. On the other hand, there are reasons for greater optimism than that. First of all, the broad outline of events from numerous sources is fairly consistent. Second, the *shura* was an accepted means of choosing a leader when there was no clear successor as a way to achieve consensus and avoid internal divisions and possible violence. Leadership in traditional Arabian society was both hereditary and elective. The thinking was that leadership was an inheritable trait, something that ran in families, but family broadly understood. On the death of a chief power passed to the surviving male relative whom the tribe regarded as possessing the greatest skill to adjudicate disputes, build alliances, and defend interests. This did not have to be the eldest son of the deceased leader. Beyond their leadership skills fortified by the consensus of the community, chiefs did not possess independent sources of coercion or force. It was the importance of group cohesion and the danger of isolation or fragmentation that gave a leader's decisions power. A *shura* was not only consistent with 'Umar's preferred way of ruling and tribal custom, but also the best way to keep everyone on board. If the six men could agree and then convince their constituents, then this was the best chance of holding the community together.

Third, despite pro-'Ali claims that he was the likely incumbent, there were also reasons why others would oppose this. A faction around 'Ali had the most coherence, and hereditary succession within Muhammad's family was neat, understandable, and took Arab lineage politics into account. It also went against the equally important emphasis on ability and consensus rather than strict inheritance. 'Ali was able to inspire incredible loyalty in some while alienating others. 'A'isha, Muhammad's favorite wife and Abu Bakr's daughter, had a long-standing grudge against him. 'Ali was not with Abu Bakr and 'Umar at the decisive meeting in which 'Umar declared Abu Bakr the first caliph. After 'Uthman's death the community rapidly divided for and against 'Ali. During his rule, 'Ali made some catastrophic decisions. While Shi'is will come to see a conspiracy against 'Ali, the Companions may have had legitimate reservations about him. It also seems reasonable, as the sources claim, that the old Meccan elite was concerned that if 'Ali became caliph leadership would become firmly ensconced in the family of Muhammad and the clan of Hashim. The Umayyads had had their wings clipped by 'Umar and no doubt wondered how much they had to do for the good of the Islamic state before they would be purged of the stain of their earlier opposition to Muhammad. 'Umar's death presented an opportunity to rebalance the scales in their favor.

Fourth, and finally, the concerns and divisions expressed in the *shura* accounts are consistent with what one would expect in light of the societal shifts engendered by Islam. This is perhaps the most important point. If we accept that they were Companions, but also men, with all of their individual and collective histories, living in a tribal society, juggling new and old loyalties, then the *shura* accounts are credible. Furthermore, the tribal divisions that animate the narratives are consistent with those that threatened the Community upon Muhammad's death, divided the Community upon 'Uthman's death, and formed the foundation of the first Islamic dynasty, the Umayyads, and after them the 'Abbasids. What seems most likely is that 'Uthman was the "best" candidate because he was a "compromise candidate"—he alone of the remaining Companions represented both the pre-Islamic tribal elite through blood and the new Islamic elite through early belief.

DEFENSE OF THE *SHURA*

The sources set out to defend the process of the *shura*—first by defending 'Umar's choice of this method. From his deathbed 'Umar arranged for the succession to be decided by a consultative council made up of six Companions of the Prophet: 'Uthman ibn 'Affan, 'Ali ibn Abi Talib, 'Abd al-Rahman ibn 'Awf, Talha ibn 'Ubaydallah, Sa'd ibn Abi Waqqas, and al-Zubayr ibn al-'Awwam. These were the surviving early converts who had remained in Muhammad's good standing throughout his life. They had also remained in Medina for much of 'Umar's reign and had been his primary advisors, especially 'Abd el-Rahman ibn 'Awf. In choosing these six 'Umar was continuing his commitment to *sabiqa*, but tribalism was present as well. All were members of different Qurayshi clans and none were from among the early Medinan converts. Politics was still the politics of lineages not individuals. While 'Uthman ibn 'Affan was from the Banu Umayya and 'Ali from the Banu Hashim, the other four were all from smaller, less powerful branches of Quraysh, as was common for early converts, including Abu Bakr and 'Umar. 'Abd al-Rahman ibn 'Awf and Sa'd ibn Abi Waqqas were both from the clan of Zuhra, the clan of Muhammad's mother. 'Abd al-Rahman was also 'Uthman's brother-in-law. Sa'd's aunt was the mother of 'Ali's uncle. Al-Zubayr was from the 'Abd al-Uzza clan, but his mother was Hashimi. Talha was not in Medina at the time and a messenger had been sent for him. These relationships and clan affiliations rather than the individual merits of the *shura* members is what the sources explore.

Various Companions asked 'Umar why he was using a consultative council instead of appointing a successor, a convenient literary device that allows 'Umar to explain himself. Authors want to defend the process in order to defend the outcome—the election of 'Uthman ibn 'Affan. 'Umar defended his choice of *shura* on three counts. First, there was no binding precedent; Muhammad did not appoint a successor while Abu Bakr did. Second, 'Umar did not want responsibility for the caliphate in death as well as in life. Third, there was no obvious candidate. 'Umar listed prominent Companions that he would gladly have chosen to succeed him, but who had already passed away. Then he appointed the six. Intriguingly, rather than praising the six individually, 'Umar points to the faults of each, but asserts that collectively they are "the best" of those who remain. For example, in one account 'Umar stated he was going to appoint 'Ali as his successor because he was "the most suitable of you to bear you along the true path" (al-Tabari, *XIV*, 144). But before he could do so he fainted (from loss of blood) and had a dream in which he was exhorted to leave the matter in God's hands. Accordingly, 'Umar settled on the *shura*. An account like this undercuts Sunni orthodoxy by its clear preference for 'Ali over 'Uthman, but it also expresses a staunchly pro-community and ultimately pro-Sunni position by asserting that the *shura* was God's idea. We can see in 'Umar's comments and guidelines a theme running through much of the material: guarded praise for 'Ali personally while defending the outcome of the *shura* politically and religiously.

'Umar is portrayed as deeply concerned that disagreements and divisions among the *shura* members would split the community. He warned 'Ali and 'Uthman, and in some versions all the *shura* members, not to favor their respective clans. He directed the *shura* members to make a decision by the end of the third day. This was not a long time and indicates fear of violence if there was not a quick resolution. It also meant that the group was not to wait for Talha. In some versions, Sa'd ibn Abi Waqqas offered to cast Talha's vote if he did not arrive in time. All of this could affect the balance of loyalties among the *shura* members. 'Umar ordered Abu Talha, one of the *Ansar* ("Helpers" from Medina) to stand guard with fifty other *Ansar* and to not let anyone disturb the *shura* members during their deliberations. This is further evidence of concern that tensions between the Qurayshi factions could turn violent. They should negotiate until there was a majority decision, and if one or two didn't agree, 'Umar urged them to submit to and support the majority. Some accounts up the ante by claiming 'Umar ordered Abu Talha to kill any recalcitrant member. The sense that force could be necessary to avert more widespread violence indicates a high level of anxiety over the durability of the community: something that became anathema to Sunni orthodoxy.

DELIBERATIONS

The *shura* members' deliberations portray a fragile communal unity threatened by tribal allegiances, personal ambitions, and mutual suspicion. The *shura* members withdrew to deliberate and confirmed all of 'Umar's worst fears. The debate became heated and voices were raised until 'Umar's son, 'Abdallah, rebuked them for their shameless bickering over the caliphate even as 'Umar lay dying. Later that day 'Umar did in fact die. They paused to bury him and again, according to some accounts, 'Uthman and 'Ali jockeyed for prominent positions during the burial. They then resumed their heated negotiations. Abu Talha reportedly wept over what these disagreements represented. None of the Companions emerge well from such descriptions.

One of the things presented as decisive to the outcome of the *shura* was that 'Abd al-Rahman ibn 'Awf somehow got into the position of casting the deciding vote. According to one version of events, 'Umar set it up this way. That is if there was a tie among the *shura* members, then all should support Ibn 'Awf's candidate. This is feasible as Ibn 'Awf was 'Umar's closest advisor and a part of the coalition of representatives from weaker Qurayshi clans. In an alternative version 'Umar did not designate Ibn 'Awf to cast the deciding vote, rather Ibn 'Awf put himself forward to play this decisive role once deliberations had begun and 'Umar was dead. In this telling, as the *shura* members argued among themselves, time was running out, and fear was growing that breakdown inside the committee would spill over into wider divisions and communal violence. 'Abd al-Rahman ibn 'Awf rebuked them for fighting over the succession, each wanting the caliphate for himself. He then proposed that one of them withdraw his candidacy in order to then choose one of those who remained to be caliph. When no one stepped forward, Ibn 'Awf offered to do so and the others agreed.

It is impossible to know for sure whether or how Ibn 'Awf came to have a deciding vote, but it is portrayed as decisive. It seems odd that 'Umar would prejudice the outcome so clearly by giving him that role. Ibn 'Awf had been a trusted advisor during 'Umar's caliphate and 'Umar may have thought Ibn 'Awf would continue 'Umar's policies of prioritizing Islamic elites over tribal elites. Perhaps 'Umar was counting on the virtue of these early Companions triumphing over lineage and clan. But then why all the warnings and precautionary procedures? Alternatively, 'Umar may not have biased the outcome at all, rather it emerged organically from the stalemate created by the competing ambitions and interests of each candidate and his respective clan.

There are two corresponding versions in the chronicles of how 'Ali responded to the *shura* arrangements. After 'Umar designated the six *shura* members and gave Ibn 'Awf the casting vote, 'Ali complained concluding that the law of lineages was going to work against him. He might have been able to count on al-Zubayr since his mother was Hashimi, but he reckoned that 'Uthman and 'Abd al-Rahman were in-laws and would nominate each other, and since Sa'd ibn Abi Waqqas was Ibn 'Awf's cousin, the three of them formed a voting bloc within the *shura* council. If Talha did not arrive in time and Sa'd got to cast his vote, or if Ibn 'Awf got the deciding vote in the case of a tie, then 'Ali was out-voted: the outcome of the *shura* was determined before it began. In the version in which Ibn 'Awf offered to remove himself to cast the deciding vote, 'Ali balked at this idea, supposedly based on the same calculation. In this version Ibn 'Awf complained to Abu Talha, who was standing guard and he urged 'Ali to go along, pointing out that Ibn 'Awf's willingness to surrender the caliphate proved he could be trusted to make the right decision. 'Ali conceded, but only after he made Ibn 'Awf swear to prioritize the truth and the good of the community and not to follow his own desires or show preference towards his kinsmen. 'Abd al-Rahman swore and then 'Ali agreed to entrust the matter to him. Even though the narrators seem keen to defend 'Umar and his choice of *shura*, the reputation of the other Companions is compromised by their ambition and bickering.

However, Ibn 'Awf came to his role, and whatever biases he may or may not have had, he is portrayed as carrying out his duties conscientiously. Anything less would have been disastrous. He consulted each of the *shura* members in turn, asking if he did not become caliph whom they would prefer. 'Uthman said 'Ali. 'Ali, Sa'd, and al-Zubayr each said 'Uthman. If 'Ali was concerned that the clan cards were stacked against him, then why did he nominate 'Uthman? Also, kinship and earlier alliances suggest al-Zubayr should have supported 'Ali. Indeed, after having expressed their initial preference for 'Uthman, 'Ali appealed to Sa'd (and al-Zubayr) to consider their own family connections with 'Ali and 'Ali's relations with Muhammad, and to not support 'Uthman (and the Umayyads) against him. The next morning Sa'd (and al-Zubayr) told Ibn 'Awf they supported 'Ali. With Talha still absent this would have given 'Ali a majority. 'Uthman emerges as the preferred candidate, but the motivations of all the participants is questionable.

Ibn 'Awf then sought the opinion of the leaders from Mecca and Medina and the garrison commanders who were all present in the city. According to some accounts they too expressed a preference for 'Uthman, or were divided between 'Uthman and 'Ali, and some elaborate on this and portray the whole community as sitting on a razor edge of tribal divisions. For example, 'Abdallah ibn Abi Rabi'a told Ibn 'Awf: "if you give the oath of allegiance to 'Ali we shall listen and disobey, and if you give the oath of allegiance to 'Uthman we shall listen and obey. So fear God, O Ibn 'Awf!" At the same time 'Ammar ibn Yasir pointed out that if Ibn 'Awf wanted all the Muslims to agree he should choose 'Ali. While another stated: "if you want Quraysh to agree, pick 'Uthman" (al-Tabari, *XIV*, 152). But 'Ammar retorted: "When did you ever give the Muslims any good advice?" The Banu

Hashim and Banu Umayya then are purported to have met to discuss the situation. 'Ammar, who had earlier spoken up for 'Ali, proclaimed the merit of those from the Prophet's family. Sa'd ibn Abi Waqqas urged Ibn 'Awf to "get it over with before our people fall into civil war" (al-Tabari, *XIV*, 152). The entire community, not just the *shura* members, were divided along tribal lines.

DECISION

Early medieval Arab historians then focus on defending the outcome. Ibn 'Awf brought 'Ali and 'Uthman before the people and asked them publicly what according to some accounts he had asked them privately the night before. This is the decisive moment of the *shura* narratives. First, Ibn 'Awf stated that if either of them was to become caliph, they should not favor their own clan. Then he asked each of them if they did become caliph would they rule based on the Qur'an, the *sunna* of Muhammad, and the deeds of Abu Bakr and 'Umar. 'Ali replied that he could not promise that, but rather that he could only hope to do so to the best of his ability and knowledge. Who, he asked, could live up to the example of the Qur'an and Muhammad. Ibn 'Awf then asked 'Uthman the same question and 'Uthman replied "yes." With that "yes" Ibn 'Awf gave 'Uthman the oath of allegiance and called the others to do the same.

Claiming that Ibn 'Awf questioned them both in the night and then brought them both forward suggests that the community had been divided in its preference for 'Uthman and 'Ali, and so Ibn 'Awf was trying one more time to get a consensus. It is possible as well that 'Ali had a smaller, but more committed number of supporters and so Ibn 'Awf wanted to "go public" to force them to submit to the majority. If he did indeed ask 'Uthman and 'Ali the same question privately, perhaps he knew that 'Ali's answer would weaken his appeal. It raises 'Uthman's election above reproach: a clear procedure led by the most venerated, surviving early Meccan converts, including consultation of the entire community, arriving at general consensus and a public promise to lead based on the Islamic pillars of Muhammad's *sunna* and the Qur'an. Indeed, this thoroughness is suspicious.

How 'Ali responded is contested in the sources which present a spectrum of options. At one end 'Ali initially refused to give the oath of allegiance, accusing Ibn 'Awf of partiality and personal ambition, declaring "you have appointed 'Uthman only so that the rule will come back to you" (al-Tabari, *XIV*, 153). 'Ali also refused on the basis that he had been deceived. This could be because Ibn 'Awf had promised to be impartial and 'Ali did not think he was. It could be because 'Ali thought the question he was asked regarding whether he would follow the Qur'an and example of Muhammad was a set up. One version goes so far as to claim 'Ali was deliberately deceived by 'Amr ibn al-'As who advised 'Ali to reply as he did and also advised 'Uthman to say what he did. In other words, 'Amr knew what 'Abd al-Rahman wanted to hear and prodded 'Uthman to give him that response. 'Ali may have been deceived, but it is hardly a vindication. Both 'Ali and 'Uthman appear willing to say anything in order to be chosen caliph. It is worth noting that 'Amr ibn al-'As will be 'Ali's nemesis in the arbitration between 'Ali and Mu'awiya in the subsequent civil war. Others also defended 'Ali and criticized Ibn 'Awf's choice and his favoritism towards the Umayya. But the *shura* members threatened to fight 'Ali while Ibn 'Awf threatened to kill him if he did not give the oath. 'Ali came back into the meeting tent and swore his allegiance to 'Uthman. Ibn 'Awf encouraged 'Ali to keep the agreement he made with God and held over him the specter of communal division. In some cases, he reinforces the point by reciting the Quranic verse 48:10: "Indeed, those who pledge allegiance to you, [O Muhammad]—they are actually pledging allegiance to Allah. The hand of Allah is over their hands. So he who breaks his word only breaks it to the detriment of himself. And he who fulfills that which he has promised Allah—He will give him a great reward." 'Ali then gave the oath. At the other end of the spectrum are accounts which assert 'Ali was supportive of 'Uthman's election and was the first or second to give him the oath of loyalty.

Ninth-century chronicles that draw together a variety of contradictory accounts frequently end with reports that insist 'Ali gave 'Uthman the oath readily. Although willing to include all the disagreements and divisions noted above, when it comes to actually giving the oath of allegiance, they present the Companions, including 'Ali, as unified and unanimous in their support for 'Uthman. This is making important assertions about 'Uthman as the rightful caliph based on the unanimous support of the Companions and the wider community confirmed by the oath of allegiance.

DEBATES

Our surviving sources were wrestling with four interlacing developments of the intervening centuries. 'Uthman's caliphate ended in regicide that led to civil war which lasted throughout the caliphate of 'Ali ibn Abi Talib. The Banu Umayya emerged victorious led by 'Uthman's cousin, Mu'awiya ibn Abi Sufyan. He established the first Islamic Dynasty, the Umayyads, who ruled from their capital Damascus until they were overthrown in the 'Abbasid Revolution. The 'Abbasids were descendants of Muhammad's uncle al-'Abbas, and fought the Umayyads in the name of the family of the Prophet, even though they were from his clan, the Hashimis, rather than his immediate family or descendants through the marriage of his daughter, Fatima, and 'Ali.

The victory of the 'Abbasids over the Umayyads meant Islamic history was no longer animated by the sibling rivalry between the two sons of 'Abd Manaf: 'Abd Shams and his descendants the Umayya, and Hashim and his descendants, including Muhammad and 'Ali. Instead the sibling rivalry was between the two grandsons of Hashim, Abu Talib and al-'Abbas, that is the Shi'i Imams and the 'Abbasid caliphs. As so often happens with successful revolutionaries, the descendants of al-'Abbas, the 'Abbasid caliphs of Baghdad, became upholders of the status quo. In defending their authority against the claims of Muhammad's descendants through 'Ali to be the true "family of the Prophet," the 'Abbasids were turned into defenders of majoritarian, consensus Islam. This meant defending the *shura* and the caliphate of 'Uthman. In other words, 'Ali and his descendants did not have a claim to the caliphate and the Companions did not make a mistake when they chose 'Uthman. It is not surprising therefore that the *shura* narratives are critical and conciliatory at the same time. A balancing act can be seen in each movement of the *shura*. Narrators categorically reject what became the Shi'i position, namely that Muhammad appointed 'Ali to be his successor. But in portraying the Companions as flawed and the community as divided, they also challenge what was becoming the Sunni orthodox view of the revered Companions.

Debates that animated ninth-century scholars and were then located within the foundation narratives for ideological heft can be seen in the speeches al-Tabari attributes to the major players. 'Uthman clearly advocates for the priority of the Companions as Muhammad's faithful supporters and rightful successors. In contrast 'Ali expresses the primacy of Muhammad's family. He stated: "Praise be to God who sent forth Muhammad as Prophet from among us and as a messenger to us. We are the house of the Prophethood, the mine of wisdom, the security of the people of the world, and a salvation for those who ask for it. We have a right; if we are given it, we take it, if we are refused it we take it by force" (al-Tabari, *XIV*, 157). This praises Muhammad's family or clan but rather than being pro-'Ali or pro Shi'i, 'Ali continues by rejecting Shi'i claims that Muhammad appointed 'Ali to succeed him. He states: "If the Messenger of God had given us a commission, we would have carried out his agreement, if he had said [something] to us [as a designation] we would have disputed [with others] over it until we die" (al-Tabari, *XIV*, 157).

Al-'Abbas is reported to have urged 'Umar to appoint 'Ali to be his successor on the grounds that 'Ali "deserves it because of his kinship to the Messenger of God, because of his marriage alliance with him, and for his being the first to have believed and to have suffered [the persecution of Quraysh]." While this appears to put forward 'Ali's merits, all the *shura* members were early converts and suffered persecution and 'Uthman married two of Muhammad's daughters. Al-'Abbas grants 'Ali rights based on kinship, but this falls far short of the Shi'i claim that Muhammad appointed 'Ali to be his successor. Indeed, nowhere do any of these accounts suggest that Muhammad appointed 'Ali. To fail to mention this is to effectively deny it. Furthermore, 'Umar reportedly rejected al-'Abbas's suggestion on the grounds that 'Ali "is idle and light spirited."

Another place where these later developments are debated is in exchanges between al-'Abbas and 'Ali. Once 'Ali saw how the family connections of the *shura* members stacked the deck against him, he complained to his uncle, al-'Abbas. Al-'Abbas, however, rebuked and reminded 'Ali that he had warned him not to participate in the *shura*, presumably on the basis that 'Ali had the superior claim which he delegitimized by his participation. Al-'Abbas had read the situation accurately and foreseen how the alignment of factions would work against 'Ali. Al-'Abbas stated that he had urged 'Ali to ask Muhammad when he was on his deathbed who was to rule after him, but 'Ali had not done it. So again, Muhammad did not designate 'Ali to be his successor. Al-'Abbas concluded: "just learn one thing from me: whenever people make you a proposal, say no, unless they are appointing you [as caliph]" (al-Tabari, *XIV*, 147). In this way al-'Abbas, the ancestor of the 'Abbasid line, is portrayed as lobbying more effectively for 'Ali's right to the caliphate then 'Ali did himself. It cleverly presents the 'Abbasids as broadly pro-'Ali while refuting the specific political claims of Shi'is based on Muhammad appointing 'Ali as his successor. Al-'Abbas continues to shift the issue away from the rights of 'Ali and his descendants to the rights of the clan of Hashim over and against the clan of Umayya. He warns 'Ali that "they" will try to push "us" out of the caliphate and if through some treachery they succeed, then no good will come of it. In this way al-'Abbas anticipates the appointment of 'Uthman, the civil war, and the rise of the Umayyad dynasty, which the 'Abbasids later overthrew, thereby restoring the rights of Muhammad's clan, the Hashimis.

Likewise, the wording of Ibn 'Awf's question to 'Ali and 'Uthman as to whether they would abide by the Qur'an and the precedent of Muhammad (and in some accounts Abu Bakr and 'Umar) reflects later developments. As argued above, the *shura* took place when the community was trying to navigate the power of pre-Islamic tribal elites while preserving the Islamic integrity of the community represented in the *sabiqa* of the *Sahaba*. With the passing of the *Sahaba*, connection to Muhammad through *hadith* would become the means of upholding and developing what was distinctively Islamic and augmenting what is in the Qur'an. There were heated debates between scholars who advocated for submission to the Qur'an and precedent and those wanting greater room for reason and innovation. The wording of 'Ali's response reflects this. 'Ali used the word "*ikhtilaf*" or "*ray*" for his own opinion; both are technical terms in juridical debates. By having 'Ali use these words while 'Uthman expressed complete submission to the Qur'an and *sunna*, the sources are connecting the choice between 'Ali and 'Uthman with ongoing discussions about the extent and basis of the ruler's authority. Ultimately, the emphasis on precedent won out, cementing the centrality of the Companions and the *hadith*.

The Companions were of critical importance to the *hadith* enterprise since they were the primary source of *hadith*. For Sunnis the edifice of Islam became predicated upon the integrity of the Companions. Could they be trusted to report what Muhammad said and did? As *hadith* solidified its position in the ninth and tenth centuries as the bedrock of Sunni Islam then so too did the Companions. This is why the narratives of the eighth and ninth centuries will be criticized later as pro-'Ali. They are pro-'Ali in the sense that they are ambivalent about 'Uthman individually and critical of the Companions collectively. This view became anathema to Sunni Muslims. But they also actively refute pro-'Ali views that became Shi'i doctrine. 'Ali was not designated by Muhammad, and the *shura* members and wider community eventually, unanimously chose 'Uthman. Nevertheless, these narratives that defend the *shura* and its outcome are criticized or rejected as pro Shi'i by the Sunni establishment because what comes in the middle, the portrayal of the Companions as divided and ambitious, became associated with Shi'i views, in other words, heresy.

'UTHMAN'S FIRST ACTS

In some ways whether the *shura* members chose wisely or not was immediately put to the test by 'Uthman's acceptance speech and his first act as caliph: handling 'Umar's murder. The chroniclers appear ambivalent. Some early accounts record 'Uthman as more or less speechless when sworn in as caliph. 'Uthman admitted that he had never been a great orator nor had he prepared anything for the occasion. Instead he refrained from saying anything for the time being, until God gave him the words. Alternatively, 'Uthman is presented as delivering a powerful sermon in which he appears gracious, humble, and seeking God's guidance as he exhorts the people towards unity and righteousness. After proclaiming the Islamic statement of faith (there is no God but God and Muhammad is His Messenger), 'Uthman asserted that "whoever obeys God and His messenger is on the right path, and whoever disobeys them has gone astray. I have succeeded as your caliph and I ask God for His assistance. If I were remote from the caliphate, it would have been better and safer for me." He then promised to follow the example of Abu Bakr and 'Umar, and beseeched God to help him and direct him towards the right course of action. He also exhorted the people "to fear God in your secret doings and your public doings and assist one another in good deeds, charity, and kinship. Do not be brothers in the open and enemies in secret" (al-Baladhuri, *Ansab al-ashraf*, 511). Similarly, in 'Uthman's accession sermon recorded in al-Tabari, the focus is entirely upon the next world as 'Uthman warns his listeners that this life, including wealth and success, is fleeting and therefore they must focus on what will endure, that is acts of righteousness. These sermons proclaim that however it came about, the Companions made a good choice when they chose 'Uthman to be the third caliph.

'Uthman's first order of business as caliph was to deliver justice for 'Umar's murder. 'Umar was killed by Fayruz Abu Lu'lu'a, a Persian slave. When he fled from the scene of the crime he was followed and killed. That could have been the end of it, but 'Umar's son, 'Ubaydallah, in a fit of grief and rage, had gone on a killing spree. In response to a rumor that Abu Lu'lu'a had been given the dagger he used against 'Umar by another Persian slave, al-Hurmuzan, and a Christian slave, Jufaynah, 'Ubaydallah attacked and killed both of them, along with Abu Lu'lu'a's daughter. He was threatening to kill others as well, but Sa'd ibn Abi Waqqas detained him and was holding him under house arrest awaiting a decision from the new caliph. Thus 'Uthman was immediately confronted with the moral quandary of what to do with 'Ubaydallah. 'Ubaydallah had not only committed murder himself, but in doing so ran the risk of splitting the community between Arabs and non-Arabs. On the other hand, his actions were crimes of passion and it seemed harsh to execute the son right after his father's murder. By some accounts 'Uthman declared a pardon for 'Ubaydallah, according to others he asked the advice of leading Meccan emigres and Medinan "Helpers". 'Ali urged him to follow the letter of the law and kill 'Ubaydallah while others urged leniency. 'Uthman chose the latter, declaring blood money be paid for al-Hurmuzan's life and that he himself would pay it. According to a third version he turned 'Ubaydallah over to al-Hurmuzan's son, stating it was his lawful right to take vengeance on 'Ubaydallah, who in turn claimed that under the circumstances he could do nothing to 'Ubaydallah and released him. The ambivalence surrounding 'Uthman's first act as caliph and how it is portrayed sets the tone for the rest of his caliphate: was he forgiving or ineffectual?

The lingering ambivalence surrounding 'Uthman and the need to defend him as a Companion rather than as an individual is clearly in evidence in a fourteenth-century trial and treatise. In 1354 a Shi'a from Hilla entered the main mosque in Damascus, refused to say the midday prayer with those gathered there and instead abused Abu Bakr, 'Umar, 'Uthman, and others, claiming they had violated the rights of the Prophet's descendants through Fatima and 'Ali ibn Abi Talib. In the subsequent trial the man was found guilty of blasphemy and summarily executed. Inspired by the trial, the Shafa'i jurist Taqi al-Din al-Subki (d. 1355) wrote a short treatise on the appropriate punishment for blasphemy against Muhammad and the Companions. It reveals a lingering ambivalence over the status of 'Uthman ibn 'Affan. Al-Subki concludes abuse of 'Uthman, unlike blasphemy against Abu Bakr and 'Umar, did not equal unbelief (*kufr*) which warranted the death penalty. Nevertheless, abuse of 'Uthman would still require the same punishment because it accused the Companions of lying when they chose a less qualified candidate in 'Uthman—and calling the other Companions liars is indeed an act of unbelief. So, whereas vilification of the other Companions is unbelief (*kufr*), vilification of 'Uthman is concealed unbelief (*zandaqa*) because it accuses the Companions of having agreed upon a wrong decision. The trial of the Shi'a from Hilla and the treatise by Taqi al-Din al-Subki reveal how the reputation of the Companions became foundational for Sunni orthodoxy and how their election of 'Uthman struck at the heart of their reputation. In narratives of 'Uthman's election it is the Companions as a sacred collective rather than 'Uthman as an individual that is on trial.

CONCLUSION

The portrayal of 'Uthman's election is important for three reasons. First, even though 'Uthman is on the sidelines for much of the narrative, the legacy of his caliphate is ever-present. It is clear that the narratives are designed to assess 'Uthman and his caliphate—either by defending or criticizing the Companions who elected him. Second, the sources highlight a tension between a pre-Islamic order of precedence based on biological lineage and tribal affiliation and a new order of precedence based on spiritual lineage through early conversion to Islam. There is good reason to believe that this was in fact a real division at the time and not a later explanatory device. After all, division along tribal lines was narrowly averted upon Muhammad's death and erupted into full scale civil war upon 'Uthman's death. Accordingly, these accounts give us a window into the seventh-century evolution of the Islamic community and the social context that continued to shape 'Uthman's caliphate. At the same time the sources clearly reflect subsequent ideological developments that were shaped by the consequences of 'Uthman's caliphate, especially the basis of caliphal authority and the split between Sunnis and Shi'is. Thus, the *shura*, like 'Uthman's caliphate, sits at a crossroads in the development from tribe to Islamic *umma* and from *umma* to schism.

What drove forward the *shura* proceedings was the pre-Islamic tribal structure reasserting itself. It had been squeezed "from below" by individuals who rose to prominence based on *sabiqa* and "from above" by the collective appeal for supreme loyalty to the new super-tribe of Islam. In some ways the death of 'Umar posed a similar threat to Islam as the death of Muhammad himself. What was the Islamic community going to be? Who would it benefit? Who would lead it and on what basis? What seems to have been determinative was that 'Uthman uniquely reconciled the old tribal elite and the new Islamic elite. He guaranteed the support of the Banu Umayya without compromising the primacy of Islam. 'Ali and his supporters would have to make a strong case for hereditary succession to override this alliance of interests. And over time they did just that. It remained to be seen whether 'Uthman would be able to pull off this balancing act in his policies not just his person.

Finally, the use of consultation in order to achieve consensus when there was not a clear successor was a known practice in pre-Islamic Arabian societies. However, the formalized process of 'Uthman's election set an important new precedent for the fledgling Islamic state. Appeals for a *shura* council to settle succession disputes became common. Even though hereditary kingship became the norm not long after 'Uthman's rule, Islamic political theorists formulated a role for leaders in the community as "those who loose and bind" who, as representatives of the people, should confirm the ruler. That this was more theory than practice, does not negate the significance of the principle of consultation. Since the early twentieth century it has received renewed attention by Islamic modernizers who argue true Islam has always been democratic.

4

CONQUESTS

INTRODUCTION

The commonly used title of the leader of the Muslim community in the early Islamic period was *Amir al-Mu'minin*, "Commander of the Faithful." Like "Commander-in-Chief," the *Amir al-Mu'minin* was ultimately responsible, but not directly in charge of, military campaigns. While a significant part of Muhammad's credentials as a prophet came from victory on the battlefield, neither Abu Bakr, 'Umar, nor 'Uthman led the armies of conquest. Indeed except for 'Umar's visit to Jerusalem after its fall, there is no mention of them leaving the environs of Mecca and Medina. Yet during 'Uthman's caliphate Arabian armies advanced north, east, and west, into Anatolia, the Caucasus, Iran, Central Asia, North Africa, and the Mediterranean Sea. Arabian troops bested the Byzantines at sea and took the battle to the gates of Constantinople; the Sasanian empire, that had ruled the Iranian plateau for 400 years, came to a definitive end with the death of Emperor Yazdigird III in 652. While leadership in the field came from the governor-commanders in the provinces of Egypt, Iraq, and Syria, it was the Commander of the Believers, 'Uthman ibn 'Affan, who appointed these men, endorsed their bold initiatives, and helped secure their success by sending men and materials from different parts of the empire. The further expansion of Arabian control and governance was one of the great achievements of 'Uthman's caliphate.

However, continuing the campaigns of conquest also put considerable strain on 'Uthman, the government, and the fighting men.

Needing able men whom he could trust, 'Uthman appointed members of the old Meccan elite and of his own clan of Umayya to key leadership positions. To some this appeared to be a reversion to a pre-Islamic tribal order and they held it against 'Uthman. 'Uthman also allowed new waves of tribesmen to settle in Egypt and Iraq where they could participate in the continuing *jihad*. Tension between old-timers and newcomers ensued. Both policies meant that those who had opposed Muhammad longest were now reaping the benefits of the conquests at the expense of those who had converted earlier and fought harder. Finally, Muhammad, Abu Bakr, and 'Umar had delivered a series of stunning military successes. Victory on the field of battle had become central to the ideological legitimacy and economic viability of the caliphate. But by the end of 'Uthman's reign the new navy was destroyed and Arabian forces were stalled in North Africa and central Asia, defeated in eastern Anatolia, and wiped out in the Caucasus. The symbolic, administrative, and financial consequences of these losses undermined 'Uthman's legitimacy as caliph.

PROBLEM OF THE SOURCES

The Muslim sources for the conquests provide us with incompatible and incomplete chronologies, written after the fact, integrated into the history of the caliphate and the triumph of Islam. The first historians sought to impose order on handed-down oral accounts by placing key events and battles within an annalistic framework. But the Muslim calendar developed long after the conquest period so there was inevitably some speculation in this. Their task was made more difficult because there were multiple campaigns in the same area and conquered cities and regions frequently rebelled, and were re-conquered, raising the risk of conflating the events of different campaigns. Nevertheless, considering that the authors were working from scraps of written and oral accounts, a century or more after the facts, their achievement is considerable.

What the Arabic sources leave wanting in terms of chronology can be met somewhat by Byzantine sources; in most cases these are contemporary or near contemporary with the events they describe and thus a century or more earlier than the extant Arabic sources. Moreover, the accounts appear within on-going chronicles with a well-established calendar. They also record Arabian defeats that Muslim sources intentionally or unintentionally omit. Unfortunately, we have no contemporary Persian histories to fill in the gaps in the Arabic sources which, considering the significance of the fall of the Sasanian empire, are surprisingly large.

Not just the chronology, but the contents of the conquest narratives frequently fail to answer some of our most basic questions. The Arabic sources emerge from an earlier tribal tradition of recording, usually orally and in poetry, the daring raids and noble acts of men of the tribe. Accordingly, they give detailed information on who led or participated in a battle or campaign and whether they did or said anything noteworthy. They say very little about military strategy, tactics, or weaponry. Furthermore, the Arabic chroniclers were not only trying to remember how an area was conquered, but defending post-conquest arrangements over who had what share in the spoils or what was the tax arrangement over a particular region or population. The Byzantine chronicles were written by and for men of the church rather than the state; the sources focus less on actual battles and more on the booty taken in battle. Nor do they care to ask why: why were the Arabians conquering the surrounding area in the first place and why were they successful. The sources generally attribute Arabian victory and Byzantine defeat to the blessing or judgment of God respectively.

The Byzantine and Arabic sources share a tendency to speak briefly of the death and destruction of the battles themselves and move quickly to the terms of surrender. This includes the immediate consequence of captives, booty, and tribute, as well as the long-term occupation and taxation. There is no doubt that the conquests, like all wars, brought death, destruction, and human suffering. Yet the persistent popular portrayal in the West of the Arab Islamic Conquests as demanding local populations convert or die has to be abandoned and indeed actively refuted. There is virtually no mention in any of the sources of invitations to convert to Islam, never mind insisting upon it. And the dead do not pay taxes. Instead what we see over and over is the offer of terms to encourage surrender and submission. Moreover, these terms varied widely depending on the relative strength of the two sides, the character of the commanders, and the surrounding conditions. What is consistent is that the more a city resisted, or if it rebelled after having submitted, then the level of death and destruction rose dramatically. As the French saying goes: *pour encourager les autres*, "to encourage the others," which was Voltaire's comment on the execution of the coward Admiral Byng. Even so, it is also possible that some accounts of rebellion and broken treaties were manufactured by the chroniclers to justify after the fact massacres and levels of violence that were later deemed un-Islamic. We simply cannot escape entirely the conundrums created by the late date of our sources.

Because the ninth-century histories of 'Uthman and his caliphate draw heavily on earlier chronicles of the conquests, the focus for much of the material on his caliphate is squarely with the armies in the provinces and on the frontiers. 'Uthman is largely unseen, but heard through correspondence and directives. The initiative for campaigns is presented as coming from the governor-commanders in the provinces, who seek and receive reinforcements from 'Uthman. At one level, even the limited involvement and communication between 'Uthman and his commanders probably reflects later levels of caliphal centralization and control projected back into this early conquest period. Nevertheless, during 'Uthman's reign the Arabians pursued the Sasanian emperor the length and breadth of the Iranian plateau and made attempts on Constantinople itself, both of which must have required 'Uthman's support. Since the sources deal more with the aftermath of battle, this is where 'Uthman appears more involved. Frequently disagreements arose over how to distribute the spoils of war between commanders and their respective forces and between the provincial garrisons and Medina. This started to chip away at 'Uthman's authority and eventually blossomed into open rebellion.

Because of the triumphalist tone and faulty dating of the conquest narratives composed after the Islamic caliphate had achieved regional dominance, defeats and setback are either forgotten, blamed on treachery in the field, or redirected towards the bravery of the fallen. As a result, the Arabic sources do not make direct links between defeat abroad and rebellion at home. We have to piece the evidence together from inferences in Arabic sources and information in Byzantine sources. But together these make clear that in addition to complaints against some of 'Uthman's appointments and policies, the military setbacks and defeats in the second half of his reign had to have lent power to those complaints. Accordingly, this chapter looks at the campaigns of 'Uthman's rule with special attention to what and how the sources claim he contributed to them, and what complaints were leveled against him in the provincial garrison centers.

NORTH AFRICA

When 'Uthman became caliph, 'Amr ibn al-'As, a charismatic and ambitious man who had led the conquest of Egypt, was serving as governor and commander there. Although Alexandria had recently rebelled and been forced to capitulate for a second time, 'Amr felt secure enough to start sending raiding parties even further west. These forces were under the command of 'Abdallah ibn Sa'd ibn Abi Sarh. 'Abdallah was an early convert to Islam and one of Muhammad's scribes, but he had then had doubts and apostatized only to later return to Islam. 'Abdallah was also 'Uthman's foster-brother. 'Abdallah led a successful campaign against the Byzantine province of Ifriqiya in what is modern-day Tunisia and eastern Algeria sometime between 645–647. Either just before or after this campaign 'Uthman removed 'Amr ibn al-'As and made 'Abdallah governor of Egypt.

Campaign

'Abdallah and his army moved west across Libya attacking Roman cities and towns along the coast that had not recovered from a conflict between the Vandals and the Byzantines in the previous century. The Byzantine province of Ifriqiya was under the leadership of the Patrician Gregory, who had rebelled against Byzantine rule, taking the local population with him. When Gregory and his troops met the advancing Arab armies, the battle lasted only a few days. Gregory fled and his army was "torn to pieces." 'Abdallah occupied 'Akuba and sent out raiding parties into the surrounding territory that carried away a large amount of booty and livestock. Having no ability to resist further, Gregory met with local leaders and decided to surrender, agreeing to pay in tribute 2,520,000 dinars. There is discrepancy in the sources as to whether the men returned to Egypt or a garrison remained. Reports that the Byzantines offered to pay in exchange for the Arabs leaving the area appear the most credible. At most a small garrison remained; the Arabs did not push further west during 'Uthman's caliphate.

Contribution

It is not clear whether 'Amr or 'Uthman initiated the Ifriqiya campaign. By one account 'Uthman initially hesitated, but after consultation (it is not clear with whom) decided to launch a direct assault on Ifriqiya and wrote to 'Abdallah ordering him to lead the attack. To ensure success 'Uthman sent a large number of reinforcements, perhaps as many as 10,000 men from around Medina: early converts from Mecca and Medina along with members of Quraysh, who were presumably late converts. But this show of support also brought its own problems. It meant that booty from the campaign would be shared more widely and with newcomers. And since those who invaded Ifriqiya did not remain there but returned to Egypt, that also meant more tribes taking a portion of the Egyptian revenue. 'Uthman complicated matters further by getting directly involved in the distribution of the booty from Ifriqiya.

Complaints

Custom was that one-fifth of the moveable booty was to be sent back to the caliph to be used to support the needy of the community, while the remaining four-fifths was distributed among the participating soldiers based on date of conversion to Islam and contribution to the battle. According to some, 'Uthman played fast and loose with the tribute money from the Ifriqiya campaign, giving a fifth of it either to 'Abdallah or to his relatives al-Hakam ibn Abi al-'As and his son, Marwan. There is no reason given for this provocative action. If true, it seems the generosity for which 'Uthman was praised as a Companion backfired during his caliphate. It also appears that 'Uthman did not distinguish between government money and his own. The reach of the caliph was still being worked out and, in the context of unprecedented wealth and an expanding central government, disagreement was probably inevitable. As we shall see in the next chapter this point became a lightning rod for opposition to 'Uthman's leadership.

Sayf ibn 'Umar tries to deflect criticism away from 'Uthman by giving a different version of events. But his account creates other inconsistencies in 'Uthman's behavior. According to Sayf, when 'Uthman sent 'Abdallah to attack Ifriqiya he told him to take for himself one-fifth out of the caliph's portion. When 'Abdallah sent the remainder of the caliph's portion on to 'Uthman, a delegation of his men complained to 'Uthman about the portion 'Abdallah had kept back for himself. It is not clear whether this was because they assumed he was stealing it without 'Uthman's knowledge or because he was receiving more than his fair share. 'Uthman assured the men that he had granted the extra one-fifth to 'Abdallah adding, however, that if they were upset by it he would have 'Abdallah give it back. The men replied that they were in fact upset, to the degree that they had lost trust in 'Abdallah and asked to have him removed from his command over them in Ifriqiya. 'Uthman wrote to 'Abdallah to return the share which 'Abdallah quickly did and then left Ifriqiya and returned to Egypt.

This is an example of Sayf ibn 'Umar working hard, but not very convincingly, to exonerate 'Uthman. 'Uthman's actions could be seen as clever incentivizing for a successful campaign. And although it diverged from precedent, both 'Uthman and 'Abdallah come across as extremely responsive to the men's complaints. But the account goes on to claim that 'Uthman compensated 'Abdallah by removing 'Amr ibn al-'As from the governorship of Egypt and giving it to 'Abdallah instead. It seems very unlikely that 'Uthman would be so sensitive to 'Abdallah's men's complaints and then give no regard to 'Amr's men. 'Amr was a capable and charismatic leader, well-regarded by the men, and his removal caused an outcry. Though on this occasion it fell on deaf ears. Other accounts claim 'Uthman made 'Abdallah the governor of Egypt before the Ifriqiya campaign, without explanation and to the great consternation of many. Alternatively, 'Uthman ordered 'Amr and 'Abdallah to share the leadership of Egypt by putting 'Abdallah in charge of taxation. But this did not work out and 'Uthman removed 'Amr and put 'Abdallah solely in charge of Egypt.

Not surprisingly, replacing the popular 'Amr ibn al-'As with a relative tainted by apostasy did not go over well. 'Amr traveled to Medina and confronted 'Uthman. 'Uthman merely responded by boasting about the amount of revenue that 'Abdallah was sending from Egypt. Al-Tabari records a memorable exchange in which 'Uthman asks 'Amr: "do you know that those she-camels have given milk plentifully since you left?" and 'Amr answered: "but their young have perished." In this telling 'Uthman favors his family and makes an enemy of a key early Companion and hero of the conquests. In 'Uthman's defense, 'Abdallah did lead a successful campaign and adopted some Byzantine practices to standardize taxation. More efficient central control meant fewer opportunities for acquiring wealth as had undoubtedly been enjoyed by the first wave of Arabian conquerors who arrived in Egypt and took advantage of the 'wild west' state of affairs. Yet 'Uthman made no effort to compensate local fighters or 'Amr. There is no excuse for 'Uthman's seeming disregard for this dimension of leadership. 'Amr ibn al-'As became a thorn in 'Uthman's side and stirred up the opposition against him, while Muhammad, Abu Bakr, and 'Umar all made efforts to make the tribal, individual, and government interests align, or at least appear to. 'Uthman repeatedly alienated and antagonized factions and individuals, giving them little reason to remain loyal. The 'Amr affair is just one example of the ways in which the link between loyalty to Islam and loyalty to the caliph, forged by Abu Bakr and 'Umar, frayed during 'Uthman's caliphate.

MEDITERRANEAN SEA

When 'Uthman became caliph, his cousin, Mu'awiya ibn Abi Sufyan, was already serving as governor-commander in Damascus. Mu'awiya was tainted by his father's fierce opposition to Muhammad and Mu'awiya himself did not accept Islam until after the fall of Mecca, surely a concession more than an act of conviction. Nevertheless, he was a talented military commander and a shrewd leader. Mu'awiya initially went to Syria under the command of his brother, Yazid ibn Abi Sufyan, during 'Umar's caliphate. When Yazid died, 'Umar expanded Mu'awiya's authority, eventually appointing him governor-commander in Damascus. He held this position when 'Uthman became caliph; 'Uthman added northern Syria and Mesopotamia to his domain. Mu'awiya was effectively in charge of the long front against the Byzantines that stretched from the Tigris River in the north east down the eastern coast of the Mediterranean.

Contribution

Mu'awiya's veteran status in the war with the Byzantines meant that he understood before anyone else that to secure the coastline the Arabs would have to neutralize the threat posed by the Byzantine navy. Mu'awiya had asked 'Umar ibn al-Khattab for permission to develop a navy, but 'Umar was reluctant. The ocean appeared threatening and other-worldly to most Arabian tribesmen more familiar with seas of sand. Moreover, it was not unreasonable for 'Umar to believe desert tribesmen had little chance of success against experienced Byzantine sailors. 'Umar wrote to 'Amr ibn al-'As, governor of Egypt, for a second opinion. 'Amr replied that it was too risky and 'Umar wrote to Mu'awiya forbidding him to pursue a navy.

When 'Uthman became caliph Mu'awiya raised again the issue of a navy, but 'Uthman refused, stating he had heard 'Umar's earlier response to Mu'awiya. A few years later Mu'awiya asked again insisting it would be easy to launch a naval campaign against Cyprus. This time 'Uthman gave the green light. He may have had a change of heart after the Byzantine army, the previous year, had been able to sail into Alexandria harbor and briefly retake the city. Also, with territory now extending along the coast of North Africa the need for a navy was becoming incontrovertible. Shipyards on the Palestinian coast and in Egypt set to work. But fear of the sea persisted; 'Uthman reportedly directed Mu'awiya not to conscript anyone, but only to take volunteers. Furthermore, as a test of Mu'awiya's confidence, 'Uthman gave his approval only if Mu'awiya was willing to have his wife sail with him, which she reportedly did when Mu'awiya set sail from Acre in the spring of 649.

Campaign

Cyprus fell without a fight. The Cypriots saw a large fleet approaching, assumed they were Byzantine and so let the ships reach land unopposed. By the time they realized their error, resistance to such a large force appeared futile and so they quickly negotiated terms of surrender. Mu'awiya and his troops entered the capital, Constantia, and then the men fanned out across the island from which they seized a rich haul of "gold, slaves, and expensive clothing." These were all divided up among the soldiers. A few days later they returned to Syria and Egypt after agreeing to the terms of tribute.

Cyprus became a condominium shared by both Byzantium and the early caliphal state. The Cypriots had to pay an annual tribute of 7,200 dinars, the same amount they paid, and continued to pay, in tribute to the Byzantines. It does not sound like an advantage to pay tribute twice, but it meant the Cypriots were not being asked to declare allegiance to the Arabians. The Arabians committed not to attack Cyprus when on expedition in the area, but they also were not obligated to defend Cyprus from attack by others. At the same time the Cypriots were not supposed to support anyone against the Arabians, but rather to inform them of Byzantine movements in the area. Cyprus could not be used as a base to launch attacks on Palestine and Syria and Mu'awiya had gotten booty, annual tribute, and a listening post in the Mediterranean. Not a bad start for the new navy.

However, the following year the Cypriots broke the terms of the agreement, allowing a Byzantine fleet to anchor off the coast while the Cypriots offered them ships and support. Mu'awiya launched a second offensive against Cyprus. The force they sent was so large (500 ships by one count) that the Byzantine fleet apparently took flight without a fight and many of the well-to-do of Cyprus left with them. Those who remained barricaded themselves into the city of Lapathos. The Arabians roamed the island killing, taking prisoners, and seizing great quantities of booty and then besieged the city of Lapathos. When it was clear that no help was coming those inside offered to surrender. Not only were the former terms and annual tribute reinstated, but Mu'awiya established a permanent settlement of 1,200 men on the island.

In the same time period Mu'awiya made an aborted attempt on Constantinople itself and then attacked the small island of Arwad just off the coast of Syria. Arwad is a tiny, rocky strip of land just two kilometers from the coastal town of Tartus. It had strategic importance in antiquity not only because of its proximity to the coast, but because of its good anchorage, consequently it was well fortified. Mu'awiya knew that he could not leave it in Byzantine hands and shortly after the fall of Cyprus he laid siege to the island. However, he was unable to take it before winter storms forced him to abandon the effort. He sent a bishop from Syria as an emissary stating if the inhabitants abandoned the island they would be allowed to depart safely for Byzantine lands. They refused and in the spring of 650 Mu'awiya returned better equipped for a sustained siege. In the ensuing negotiations the people of Arwad agreed to leave the island when Mu'awiya promised that they could settle wherever they wished, whether that be in Syria or Byzantine territory. Mu'awiya then ordered the city and its defensive walls destroyed making the island uninhabitable.

The fall of Arwad reveals the complex identities and loyalties of late antiquity. The residents of Arwad though presumably Christian and previously loyal to Byzantium felt their relationships and connections in Syria were more important; nor did they fear establishing themselves in Syria, even under Arabian Muslim control. It also shows that Mu'awiya did not perceive the residents of Arwad as posing a threat or a fifth column. He was worried about the strategic location and resources of the island that could be used by the Byzantine navy as a base for attacking Syria. The fall of Arwad also reveals some of the limitations of the Muslim Arabic accounts of the Conquests. The above account appears with slight variation in Greek, Syriac, and Christian Arabic sources whose information can be traced back to a chronicle by Theophilus bar Toma of Edessa (d. 785). This relatively early date, but more importantly the absence of ideological polemic and the presence of accurate geographic details point to a high level of reliability. In contrast the earliest Muslim source by Ibn A'tham of Kufa (d. 858) reveals that the author has virtually no sound information about the Arwad campaign, beyond the fact that the island was captured by an Arab fleet sent by Mu'awiya when he was governor of Syria. Instead it seems clear that fragments of information that made little sense to someone in ninth-century Iraq who knew nothing of Syria or its coastline were padded out with stereotypes and storytelling. For example, a captured Byzantine was reportedly brought to Mu'awiya and then offered to show them the way to a large island, and when he did so the Arab forces were able to take the islanders by surprise and slaughtered many residents. Of course, none of this makes sense since Arwad was barely a mile off the coast and both it and an approaching fleet would have been clearly visible to all. Instead the fall of Arwad provides merely a setting to relate a tale of Byzantine treachery and Arab bravery. And while Arwad presents a warning when it comes to handling the sources, since it became an abandoned strip of land lacking any strategic or financial significance and difficult to envisage from Iraq, it should also be taken as an extreme example.

The fall of Cyprus and Arwad were strategic and symbolic triumphs that gave notice to the Byzantines. While Mu'awiya deserves the credit for the idea and the success of the new navy, it is also right to recognize 'Uthman. Mu'awiya could not have acted without 'Uthman's support. The navy was one of the great innovations of 'Uthman's reign. Launching a navy opened a new front in the ongoing war with Byzantium, punctuated by the attempt on Constantinople itself. This showed the Muslim resolve to replace Byzantium as the regional superpower.

IRAN

Arabian victory over the Sasanian army at the Battle of Nihawand in 642 opened the Iranian Plateau to Arabian forces. Iran's mountainous terrain and the Great Salt Desert in east-central Iran meant that the Arabians pursued three routes of conquest. Troops based in Basra, where the Tigris River enters the Persian Gulf, were responsible for one front which extended east and south along the edge of the Persian Gulf and the Gulf of Oman, and then north-eastward into Afghanistan. A second front was manned by troops out of Bahrain who crossed the Persian Gulf by boat and headed eastward towards India. A third was north-eastward between the Alborz Mountains and the salt desert. Troops in the garrison city of Kufa in central Iraq took the lead on this front. In the mountainous region around the Caspian Sea it is perhaps more accurate to speak of incursions rather than conquest.

During 'Uthman's reign the Iranian plateau was subdued and the Sasanian emperor killed. Although the outermost reaches of the Islamic empire shifted dramatically north-eastward, to the city of Merv, we have surprisingly little information about how this was achieved. Many Persian cities surrendered on the understanding that the Arabians would not take captives or booty and the local population would pay the poll tax and the land tax. With the Sasanian empire in disarray and the emperor on the run, local leaders opted to switch their allegiance and continue their role much as before, but now in suzerainty to the Arabians rather than the Sasanians. In a decade the Arabians defeated the Sasanians and controlled all of their former territory, not just in central Iran, but western Afghanistan and Turkmenistan. The Arabians had secured tribute from the major cities and controlled most of the major trade routes. But no new Muslim cities or garrison towns were created, there was no migration of Arabians into the area at this time, and no great mosques were built. The Arabians exercised minimal influence beyond controlling trade routes and collecting taxes and if the opportunity arose local leaders resisted even this.

NORTHERN IRAN AND THE CAUCASUS

Northern Sasanian territory around the Caspian Sea had been invaded during 'Umar's rule and the local population forced to pay tribute. But upon 'Umar's death they rebelled and stopped paying. Early in

'Uthman's caliphate the men of Kufa set out to retake the area. The garrison in Kufa had grown to a reported 40,000 fighters; 10,000 a year would go out on campaign, 4,000 to Tabaristan, and 6,000 to Azerbaijan. In this way men would rotate and fight on the frontier every fourth year. Al-Walid ibn 'Uqba led the raids into Azerbaijan to retake the territory, and extract submission and tribute a second time. The information on this campaign is especially confusing, most likely because the details of multiple campaigns over many years to take and retake different cities became conflated over time. Al-Walid and his commanders went into the land "killing and taking prisoners and booty" and one of al-Walid's commanders returned to al-Walid with "his hands laden with plunder." Al-Walid defeated the people of Azerbaijan again and re-imposed the terms of before, namely the payment of 800,000 dirhams in tribute. The terms he made with them stipulated that in addition to tribute they had to pay the land tax and the poll tax, but in exchange the Arabians would not interfere with their possessions, inviolable rights, or children. After the campaign in Azerbaijan al-Walid withdrew to Mosul. Al-Ashath ibn Qays al-Kindi, one of the leaders in the *Ridda* Wars against Abu Bakr, was left in charge of Azerbaijan.

Contribution

When 'Uthman became caliph he removed 'Umar's commander-governor in Kufa and appointed Sa'd ibn Abi Waqqas, a veteran of the campaign against the Sasanians and a member of the *shura* council that had elected 'Uthman. A year later 'Uthman removed him and appointed his own half-brother al-Walid ibn 'Uqba. Al-Walid had led the successful campaign in Azerbaijan and was clearly an able leader. This may have been why 'Uthman promoted him. However, he was also a controversial figure; 'Uthman's half-brother was known for drunkenness and other moral lapses. A few years later, in 649 or 650, 'Uthman removed al-Walid and appointed Sa'id ibn al-'As as governor of Kufa. Al-Walid was brought down by a number of personal scandals that we shall look at in more detail in the following chapter. Sa'id was 'Uthman's maternal cousin.

Campaign

In the mountainous regions in the north-east the Arabians fought city by city, mountain fortress by mountain fortress. These campaigns were under the direction of Sa'id ibn al-'As. Around 649 Sa'id ibn al-'As set out on campaign south of the Caspian Sea, heading for Khurasan. At the same time 'Abdallah ibn 'Amr with troops from Basra was making his way from the south-east, also headed for Khurasan. 'Abdallah reached the area first and laid siege to Nishapur in north-eastern Iran. Sa'id got word of this and so rather than continuing east turned north and besieged the town of Tamisah on the shore of the Caspian Sea. The people vowed to surrender if Sa'id promised not to kill a single man. Sa'id agreed and when the townspeople surrendered he killed all the men except one, thereby keeping to the letter of his promise. Sa'id made peace with the people of Jurjan to the east of the Caspian Sea and they agreed to pay an annual tribute. It is not clear whether Sa'id led this campaign after he became commander of the garrison in Kufa or whether 'Uthman gave him that position as a reward for this successful campaign. But the success was short lived. Some years the people of Jurjan would pay 300,000 dirhams and others only 100,000, claiming to have fulfilled their treaty obligations. Then they rebelled and stopped paying entirely. Not only were Kufan forces unable to retake the territory, but the road became too dangerous for them to pass. The way east from this northern direction remained closed until an Umayyad general conquered the area half a century later.

Complaints

Kufa became a center of opposition to 'Uthman. This is not blamed directly on the tough fighting conditions or military setbacks, but on conditions in Kufa itself. But the two were related. After the initial campaign in Azerbaijan, Kufan troops met with few victories and thus little booty. Furthermore, apparently in an effort to make progress on this front, 'Uthman had allowed tribes from Arabia to move into Kufa to participate in the *jihad* in northern Iran. But since Arabians did not establish permanent settlements in this territory, those tribes remained in Kufa, swelling the number of people demanding a portion of the wealth generated in the local area, even though they had played no role in the conquest of Iraq. The system set up by 'Umar was predicated upon and created the expectation for continual expansion.

THE IRANIAN PLATEAU

The other major thrust against the Sasanians was based out of Basra. The garrison in Basra had been established by Abu Musa al-Ash'ari, an early Companion of Muhammad from Yemen. When 'Uthman became caliph he retained Abu Musa al-Ash'ari as the governor-commander there. The forces based out of Basra had moved into Fars, that is the central Iranian plateau and heartland of the Sasanian empire. Some cities were quickly defeated while others resisted for a time. Some submitted and paid tribute, but then stopped doing so when they had managed to reinforce their position. Abu Musa and his forces were continually taking or retaking the major cities. Rugged geography helped the Sasanians, but ultimately could not make up for the loss of the Sasanian army. While there were occasions in which the troops met fierce resistance and inclement weather, the impression is that much of this territory "fell" to Arabian control because local elites surrendered with little resistance in order to get better terms. By 650 most of Iran had been pacified, with the capital, Istakhr, one of the last holdouts. This was the birthplace of the Sasanian royal line and the emperor Yazdigird III had made his way there in the hopes that he would likely find the greatest support. He was not mistaken, the inhabitants put up a fierce fight and held out even as surrounding cities fell.

Contribution

'Uthman is described appointing the leaders of different expeditionary forces and then all the commanders of the different provinces within the Sasanian empire as they fell to Arabian forces. In 649 things came to a head in the campaign against the vestiges of the Sasanian empire that elicited a broader restructuring. 'Uthman removed Abu Musa from Basra, and recalled and appointed 'Abdallah ibn 'Amir in his place. He was 'Uthman's maternal cousin who he had earlier put in charge of Sijistan. 'Uthman greatly increased the territory and men under 'Abdallah's command, adding the territory and men who had been fighting in the third front in the far east of the empire. This centralized command and enlarged force was intended to strike the final blow against Yazdigird and the Sasanian holdouts. This appears to have been a well-judged strategic intervention and 'Abdallah was able to close out the campaign in Iran.

Even so, removing Abu Musa, a highly respected early Companion, and replacing him with his own 25-year-old cousin was not without controversy. On the one hand Abu Musa was old and clearly lacked dynamism and initiative; he had failed to take the Sasanian capital of Istakhr and eliminate Yazdigird and the remnants of Sasanian resistance. There were rumors as well that the Qurayshi tribesmen were not happy about serving under an Ash'ari and would serve better and fight harder for one of their own. It was in recognition of this that 'Uthman appointed 'Abdallah, a shrewd young man who had already proven his tactical and leadership abilities. Sayf ibn 'Umar gives another, somewhat implausible reason, which suggests that there were murmurings against the appointment. Sayf presents 'Uthman's appointment of 'Abdallah as a response to the complaints of the people and an effort to uphold a high Islamic moral standard. He claims that when Kurds rebelled in western Iran in the third year of 'Uthman's rule, Abu Musa called upon the people of Basra exhorting them to wage *jihad* and put down the Kurdish rebellion. But when Abu Musa prepared to set forth with all his baggage loaded on mules he expected the men to march on foot. In response some of them refused to comply and instead complained to 'Uthman. Supposedly, this was why 'Uthman removed Abu Musa, but this appears to be an effort by Sayf to exonerate 'Uthman and make his appointment appear to be a response to the will of the people. In the process, however, he reveals that 'Uthman was criticized and needed to be defended.

Campaign

In 650 'Abdallah's men took Istakhr and the surrounding area after a long siege that, unusually, included the use of siege engines. When the city finally fell many of its inhabitants were massacred, perhaps as many as 40,000 people, including Sasanian elite from other areas who had sought refuge in the city. The death and destruction at Istakhr were unlike anything else in the conquest of the Iranian plateau. There are reports that the city surrendered and then broke the terms of the surrender and rebelled. This may be why the destruction was so absolute, though it may also have been a calculated effort to destroy the political and religious center of the Sasanian empire and prevent it becoming a center of opposition to Arabian rule. Nevertheless, Yazdigird III managed to escape from Istakhr and 'Abdallah ibn 'Amir pursued him from the south-west edge of the Sasanian empire all the way to its north-eastern province of Khurasan. Along the way the Arabians had to contend with the terrain and climate as much as the people. At least one force was wiped out in a snowstorm. Most towns surrendered to avoid destruction, while walled or fortified cities were more likely to resist, but eventually these too surrendered agreeing to pay tribute in gold and slaves. Yazdigird III made it as far as Merv, in what is today Turkmenistan. Along the way he had tried to rally support, but the elite of Iran had concluded it was in their interest to come to an accommodation with the Arabians.

In Merv Yazdigird expected to be joined by Khurrazad, the Median prince from western Iran. But then Khurrazad changed his mind and decided to not join up with Yazdigird because of a disagreement over strategy. Yazdigird wanted to head east and garner support from the Turks and Chinese to wage a counter-assault on the Arabians. Khurrazad did not want to abandon his people to Arab depredations and did not think they would get much from the Turks and Chinese when they had nothing to offer in return. Like many other leaders in the region, he concluded the best option was to come to terms with the Arabians and then see what opportunities might arise in the future to maximize independence or throw off Arabian control entirely. Abandoned, Yazdigird's much weaker force was eventually overtaken and defeated by the Arabians. Yazdigird managed once again to escape. However, he was killed shortly thereafter not by an Arabian, but by one of his own subjects, under mysterious circumstances. The most widely accepted version of events is that Yazdigird had been haughty towards the governor of Merv, Mahawayh, who had then expelled Yazdigird from the city. Yazdigird hid in a mill near the city gate, but was discovered by the miller who killed him and took his head to Mahawayh, presumably expecting to be rewarded. An ignominious end to the great Sasanian empire if ever there was one. News of Yazdigird's death had ripple effects across the Near East. His son, Parviz III, did make his way east, appealed to the Turks and Chinese for troops to fight the Arabians, and managed to carve out a territory for himself in eastern Iran, taking advantage of the chaos of the first Arab Civil War (656–660). But after that the Arabians managed to push him back into China where he died in 680.

No Complaints

After the death of Yazdigird III there is no mention of pushing farther north or east; one imagines there was a need to consolidate control over the territory already taken. The Arabians also appear to have been stymied for a time by the fierce conditions and fighters they encountered in and around Kabul. Somewhat surprisingly, there is no mention of major Arab settlement or building within Iran and it seems life continued much as it had before, but with different tax collectors. The stable revenue from this region, additional booty after putting down a rebellion, and the small garrison forces stationed throughout seems to have kept the tribesmen in Basra busy and content. Unlike the other garrison cities, the tribes based in Basra continued to make territorial gains through most of 'Uthman's caliphate. The complaints coming out of Basra were commensurably more muted. Furthermore, joining the two armies fighting in eastern Iran meant that 'Abdallah did not need reinforcements from Kufa or Syria. Nor is there mention of subsequent waves of tribesmen moving into Basra as they did in Kufa. Thus, the tribes in Basra had a different experience of the conquests and this meant they had a different experience with 'Uthman.

ARMENIA

Armenian historic lands extended well beyond the current country of Armenia into modern-day eastern Turkey, northern Iran, and Iraq, along a frontier zone between the Persian and Byzantine empire. As Christians they were more closely allied with the Byzantines, but the Armenians also had their own internal divisions, and in their rivalries would seek different backers. These divisions also prevented the Armenians from organizing a unified resistance to the Arabian forces when they entered Armenian territory during 'Umar ibn al-Khattab's caliphate. At the same time, unlike Syria and Palestine, the local population was armed; this, along with the challenging terrain and weather, gave the Armenians advantages not held by other Byzantine territories in their confrontation with the Arabians.

The Arabians had made two incursions into Armenian territory during the reign of 'Umar. In the first, were Syrian troops under the leadership of Habib ibn Maslamah al-Fihri. They had persevered as winter set in, surprising the Armenian defenders, and capturing the important city of Dvin, "putting many of its residents to the sword and carrying off many captives and riches." A second campaign in 643 ended with Arabian defeat and retreat. Theodore Reshtuni, the Byzantine-approved commander in Armenia, launched a surprise attack on the Arabs. Out of 3,000 elite fighting men only a few escaped. Theodore sent 100 of the best Arab horses to the Byzantine emperor as a gift and to announce the glory of his victory. When 'Uthman became caliph, the Arabians tried to retake Armenian territory, but the climate and terrain were a challenge and the people well-defended. The Arabians departed with little.

Campaign

In 653, perhaps influenced by word of the death of Yazdigird III, Theodore Reshtuni abandoned his alliance with the Byzantines and signed an agreement with Mu'awiya. The Armenians did not have to pay tribute for three years and after that could pay whatever they thought fair. In exchange for local autonomy and the absence of Arabian troops, they were required to maintain 15,000 cavalry to support the Arabians if needed. Mu'awiya may have agreed to these terms because of the rugged conditions and well-defended population that had thwarted the Arabians previously. Mu'awiya, perhaps also inspired by Yazdigird's death, had begun to prepare for another attempt on Constantinople. This may have pushed him to secure his eastern flank in Armenia. Apparently unwilling to lose Armenian suzerainty without a fight, the Byzantine emperor Constans II personally led a Byzantine force into Armenian territory in 653. However, word of the pending naval assault prompted Constans II to return to Constantinople, leaving the Byzantine army behind under the command of the Patrician Marianus. News of this approaching force prompted 'Uthman to order Mu'awiya to send Habib Ibn Maslama al-Fihri to support Reshtuni. He set out with 6,000–8,000 men. Together they defeated the Byzantines. Habib killed Marianus and his men plundered the Byzantine camp.

Contribution

'Uthman appears to have been more involved in the Armenia campaign than he was in Iran. There are several possible explanations for this. While the Sasanian government never recovered from the defeat at Nihawand and was finally defeated a decade later, the Byzantines did recover from the defeat at Yarmuk; they retained their capital and control of vast territory, and they were able to man an army and a navy. The Byzantines continued to rule for another 800 years. In addition, Armenia was between Mu'awiya's jurisdiction in northern Mesopotamia and Sa'id ibn al-'As's in central Iraq. 'Uthman directed Mu'awiya to send Habib and 6,000–8,000 men into Armenia. Habib then wrote to 'Uthman asking for additional reinforcements and 'Uthman wrote to Sa'id ibn al-'As in Kufa ordering him to send a force under Salman ibn Rabi'a-l-Bahili to support Habib. Accordingly, Salman set out at the head of 6,000 Kufans. However, the battle was over before they arrived. Nevertheless, the Kufan troops demanded a share in the booty, apparently because they had marched all that way and refused to leave empty-handed. Not surprisingly, the Syrian troops refused. The dispute between Habib and Salman escalated and they wrote to 'Uthman to adjudicate. 'Uthman wrote back stating the spoils belonged by right to the Syrians. While this was a reasonable conclusion it is not hard to imagine the Kufans' frustration. Salman ibn Rabi'a and his troops were then sent north-east along the western coast of the Caspian Sea to confront the Khazar tribesmen there. The extent to which this was to take new territory or just make sure the Kufans had something to show for their effort is impossible to determine. The Kufans made it past the fortress city of Balanjar, but were then ambushed by the Khazars; there was no easy escape route in this mountainous region and the Arabian force was largely destroyed; only a few made it back to Kufa.

Complaints

The Arabic sources do not make a direct connection between the defeat at Balanjar and growing opposition to 'Uthman at home. But Sayf ibn 'Umar's treatment of the battle is full of evil omens and eulogies for the fallen that convey the psychological blow of this defeat. He also hints that the defeat was God's judgment for commanders in the field, such as al-Ash'ath ibn Qays a-Kindi, who despite leading forces against the Muslims in the *Ridda* Wars, and thus a former apostate, was made governor of Azerbaijan by 'Uthman. The lament and thinly veiled criticism may be as close as the sources can come to acknowledging that a major defeat could rock the confidence of the Arabs or the legitimacy of the caliph. To do so directly was simply incompatible with the vision of a triumphant Islam, ordained and sustained by God, that existed by the time the Conquest narratives were written.

MEDITERRANEAN SEA

Campaign

The death of Yazdigird in 652 may also have emboldened Mu'awiya to make another attempt on Constantinople. This was the naval campaign that had called Emperor Constans II to withdraw from Armenia. Mu'awiya prepared for two years with shipyards along the Levantine coast and in Alexandria working hard to produce a fleet worthy of the endeavor. The greatest naval battle of 'Uthman's reign is known as the Battle of the Masts or the Battle of Phoenix in 655. A great fleet under the command Ibn Sa'd engaged the Byzantine fleet, commanded by the Byzantine emperor himself, off the coast of south-western Turkey. Arabic and Byzantine sources give more details than usual that point to the scale and significance of the battle. They had to contend with strong winds, but when the fleets met the Arabians lashed their ships to the Byzantines' and fierce fighting waged across the decks. By turning the battle from one of ships at sea to one of hand-to-hand combat on solid ground, the Arabians were able to play to their strengths. It also meant there was no way to withdraw and the fighting was particularly fierce and the casualties high. In one description they fought "until the blood was washed up on the shore by the pounding waves; the breakers threw up men's corpses in heaps." However, it was the Byzantines who lost more men and most of their ships; the emperor himself barely managed to escape. He made his way back to Constantinople. This was just as well because the Arabians decided to press their advantage, continued up the Aegean Sea, and besieged Constantinople. According to a contemporary of the events, Sebeos, God finally intervened on behalf of the Byzantines and a great storm arose and smashed the Arabian fleet. At the same time, a supporting army that Mu'awiya had stationed in the center of Anatolia, near Cappadocia, was defeated by the local Byzantine garrison and forced to flee to northern Mesopotamia for safety.

Contribution and Complaints

The Arabic sources do not mention 'Uthman in relation to this campaign—neither in contributing to the important victory at the Battle of the Masts nor in criticizing him for the subsequent defeat. As a matter of fact, Arabic sources do not mention the attempt on Constantinople and its corresponding defeat. This may again be because it was inconsistent with the carefully cultivated portrayal of the Conquests by the time the narratives reached their final form two centuries later. Instead they focus on the victory at the Battle of the Masts. However, as with the defeat at Balanjar, the Arabic sources do make a link between the naval campaign and growing opposition to 'Uthman. They shift from the victory of the Battle of the Masts not to the defeat of Constantinople, but to criticism within the Muslim ranks against 'Uthman for abuses back home. These came not from the Syrian troops, but from troops stationed in Egypt that participated in the campaign. This may also point to the careful crafting of the narratives after the fact since Mu'awiya and the Syrians who rose to power demanding justice for 'Uthman's murder could hardly be seen as participating in the rebellion against him. In contrast Egypt was a well-known center of opposition to 'Uthman.

As is common in the Arabic sources, the conflict is personalized, and in this case projected on to two key critics of 'Uthman in Egypt, Muhammad ibn Abi Hudhayfa and Muhammad ibn Abi Bakr, the son of the first caliph. In one version of events, when 'Abdallah ibn Abi Sarh tried to lead prayers on board one of the ships, Muhammad ibn Abi Hudhayfa spent the time shouting from the back "God is greatest!" Afterwards 'Abdallah sought him out and rebuked him and told him not to do it again; Muhammad defended his right to proclaim the greatness of God and indeed did so again during the next corporate prayer. 'Abdallah threatened to arrest him, but admitted he did not know if 'Uthman would support this. Instead he prohibited Muhammad from sailing with them. Muhammad ibn Abi Hudhayfa sailed into the battle as the only Muslim on a ship manned by Egyptian Christians. After the victory, on the return journey, Muhammad pointed out that there was another *jihad* waiting for them back home—namely the fight against the abuses of 'Uthman ibn 'Affan. "He continued until he had corrupted the people. By the time they approached their own country he had corrupted them, for they were openly saying things that they had not [previously] uttered." A variant version places Muhammad ibn Abi Bakr, the first caliph's son, with Muhammad ibn Abi Hudhayfa and adds that they fought the most feebly. The two Muhammads defended their poor performance on the grounds that 'Abdallah ibn Abi Sarh did not have legitimate authority over them because he was appointed by

'Uthman who had committed various abuses. We turn to these in the next chapter.

CONCLUSION

There is a general sense that the Conquests put a strain on 'Uthman as a leader and on the as yet inchoate government structures. Although only recently conquered, Egypt, Syria, and Iraq appear incredibly stable. The local population does not resist Arabian rule. The challenge came not in subduing the populace, but in subduing the tribal leaders. The skills needed to conquer a territory are rarely the same ones needed to govern it. How much autonomy were provincial leaders to have over local government and revenue? In addition, the allocation of land and the distribution of tax revenue is a different calculus than for moveable goods seized as booty. Problems came not from the local population rising up, but from the conquering tribes settling down.

'Umar had replaced governors from time to time, presumably to prevent them from developing an independent support base in the areas they governed or when they exhibited un-Islamic behavior. 'Uthman also appointed new governors; however, he would be criticized for they were all close relatives. A power struggle was brewing between leadership based on early conversion to Islam and the authority of the old Meccan elite. Balancing the interests of the old and new order had been an issue from the beginning of Islam. But unlike his predecessors, 'Uthman seems to have been unable to navigate this. Not only did he consolidate power in the hands of his extended family, he made no effort to soften the blow or compensate different interest groups. Despite the rapidly changing circumstances in which he sought to rule, it is hard to not find him deficient as a leader. But as the one whom the Companions chose to be caliph and therefore by extension God's chosen, 'Uthman's management of the Conquests became another facet of the "problem of 'Uthman."

These domestic administrative challenges were exacerbated by the ideological and financial necessity of continuing *jihad* against the Byzantines and the Sasanians. In the latter years of 'Uthman's rule,

Arabian forces were stalled or defeated on every major front. This was not 'Uthman's fault, but he would certainly suffer most from it. It meant troops in the provinces were not rewarded with fresh waves of booty, and that the growing tribal populations in the provinces had to learn how to govern rather than conquer and share the existing revenue. The entire Islamic edifice was also based upon the premise that God rewarded the faithful with victory. If they were not victorious then someone was not being faithful. Who could be more responsible for that than the Commander of the Faithful? Accordingly, the loss of confidence on the front offered an ideological match to the growing discontent with 'Uthman.

5

CRISIS

INTRODUCTION

We have come to the heart of the "problem of 'Uthman"— the accusations of abuse that led to rebellion and regicide. 'Uthman was tasked with governing a greatly expanded empire even as the pace of the conquests stalled to a near halt. This meant there was not the same windfall from the spoils of war, but rather the hard slog of collecting taxes from a majority population of non-Muslim agriculturalists and city dwellers and then allocating that revenue. In this context some key questions came to the fore. What should be the relationship between the provincial capitals and Medina? What was the authority of the caliph over revenue and rituals? What should be done with surplus wealth? Did the rewards of the conquests belong to the conquering tribes in perpetuity? Where could able and loyal leaders be found, especially as the Companions were aging and dying? What was the relationship between loyalty to the caliph and loyalty to Islam? Governing a large empire required leaders with administrative ability; was this more important than the religious conviction and fighting spirit initially needed to guarantee the survival of the movement? The answers to these questions were bound to produce conflict.

There is considerable consistency in the early sources in terms of 'Uthman's problematic policies, the response to them, and the events of the rebellion. Even Ibn Sa'd (d. 845), author of the first biographical dictionary whose entries provide a template for conservative orthodox

Sunni Islam, and whose narrative of 'Uthman clearly censors the most damning accounts, acknowledged a few central abuses. He states that during the first six years of 'Uthman's caliphate no one held anything against him, but 'Uthman was more beloved by Quraysh because he was not as strict with them as 'Umar had been. Moreover, in the last six years of his reign he "became slack in his affairs" and appointed members of his family and his house to government posts "and he gave to Marwan a fifth [of the booty from the conquest] of Egypt, and gave his relatives money, and borrowed from the treasury." Ibn Sa'd leaves out a lot to be sure, and even takes liberties in this brief summary since 'Uthman's controversial appointments began shortly after he took office. Nevertheless, these events are not disputed and clearly something went wrong for 'Uthman to be killed.

Most chroniclers position 'Uthman on a spectrum between villain and victim depending on the level of blame they place on 'Uthman personally, his advisors, circumstances, and unintended consequences. There is also a counter-narrative that portrays 'Uthman as a saint and martyr that will be addressed in the next chapter. In the narratives that are critical of 'Uthman there are efforts to deflect criticism away from some characters and on to others. For example, 'Ali is frequently presented as walking a fine line between warning 'Uthman based on Quranic principles and remaining scrupulously loyal to 'Uthman. This seems carefully calibrated to praise 'Ali and distance him from the revolt against 'Uthman, as any role in it would delegitimize his own succession to the caliphate. At the same time the sources are reticent to criticize Mu'awiya or the tribes based in Syria. Instead, these pillars of the Umayyad dynasty appear as exemplars of stability and strong leadership. On the other hand, once the rebellion began there is a clear effort to shift blame from 'Uthman on to Marwan ibn al-Hakam, 'Uthman's key advisor. Marwan was 'Uthman and Mu'awiya's cousin, the Umayyad caliph whose descendants ruled from Damascus until they were overthrown in the 'Abbasid Revolution of 750. Sources juxtapose Marwan's consistently bad advice and nefarious meddling with 'Ali's sound advice and commitment to justice and unity. Furthermore, most of our sources are from Iraq, especially Kufa, which became the center of opposition to the Umayyad dynasty and birthplace of Shi'ism. All of this should alert us to the ways in which the sources are taking ideological positions influenced by the political and sectarian milieu that the rebellion against 'Uthman helped create.

Looking at 'Uthman's policies, he had the difficult task of not only keeping the conquests going, but of incorporating and governing the conquered lands. As we saw with 'Uthman's election, sources are often more interested in praising 'Umar than in defending 'Uthman, and may even sacrifice the latter to save the former. Although 'Umar's ten-year rule saw incredible successes, he also left 'Uthman with some real challenges. As discussed in the previous chapter, first and foremost was an expectation that the Muslim state would continue to experience success on the battlefield. Administratively, 'Umar initiated policies of greater centralization when he set up the registry for allocating war booty and stipends, but the job of further integrating conquered lands and annual tax revenue fell to 'Uthman. 'Umar had offered redemption to and relied upon tribes from central and eastern Arabia who had rebelled against Abu Bakr in the *Ridda* Wars to provide the manpower for the conquest of Iraq. These tribes continued to agitate against Medina and Quraysh; 'Uthman had to constrain their secessionist tendencies. Abu Bakr had responded to those who tried to separate loyalty to Islam and loyalty to the caliph by calling it apostasy and waging the *Ridda* Wars. While 'Uthman's reactions to criticism are portrayed as excessive, it is possible that he did respond harshly because he saw in those acts of disobedience the seeds of schism, *fitna*—as some sources claim.

The task 'Uthman faced would have taxed the greatest of leaders, but as we have seen from his behavior as a Companion during the consultative council that chose him to be caliph and the Conquests, he was a gentle and generous family man, and not a particularly astute or active leader. He relied heavily on others to take the initiative and reacted to rather than anticipated events. He also failed to keep ambitious individuals or tribal factions convinced that loyalty to Islam meant loyalty to the caliph. 'Uthman seems to have either thought newly elevated tribes would defer to the old tribal hierarchy or he completely misunderstood how his "generosity" to his family would appear to those anxious to protect their new-found position and prestige. Furthermore, where 'Uthman did take the initiative—giving generously to his family, performing the prayers on pilgrimage, and codifying the circulating Quranic texts—he opened himself up to accusations of "changing" Islam.

His election and the conquests portray 'Uthman surrounded by more dynamic leaders. They promoted 'Uthman as a compromise candidate, a buffer between personal and group rivalries. They then took advantage of dissatisfaction with him, and the state of affairs in the empire, to further their personal and tribal interests. Most did little to save him. The problem of 'Uthman is that he poses a problem for the image of the Companions, who appear divided, seeking their own advantage at the expense of 'Uthman and the unity of the Community.

The image that emerges from the early sources is that 'Uthman's caliphate was characterized by favoritism and corruption that led to divisions between the Companions, between the tribes, and between the center and the periphery. It is hard not to conclude that 'Uthman was not the right person for the job. But this is exactly the core problem. If 'Uthman was not the right person for the job why did God let him become caliph? Considering the catalog of abuses of power leveled against an early Companion of the Prophet, chosen to be caliph by other early Companions, and the divisions that ensued, 'Uthman was a test of the entire edifice of Islam. If Muhammad's life and message had no material impact on this first generation of Believers, what truth was in it?

COMPLAINTS

Relatives

'Uthman consolidated power in the hands of his family and clan, the Umayya of Mecca. As discussed in the previous chapter, 'Uthman appointed family members as commander-governors in the garrison towns in Egypt, Iraq, and Syria. He retained Mu'awiya, his cousin, in Syria-Palestine and expanded his territory into northern Mesopotamia. In Egypt, 'Uthman dismissed 'Amr ibn al-'As as governor and appointed his own foster-brother, 'Abdallah ibn Sa'd ibn Abi Sarh. In the garrison city of Kufa in central Iraq, 'Uthman appointed Sa'd ibn Abi Waqqas from the *shura* council, but a year later he removed Sa'd and appointed his half-brother, al-Walid ibn 'Uqba. In response to complaints against al-Walid, 'Uthman replaced him with another relative, his cousin, Sa'id ibn al-'As. In Basra in southern Iraq, 'Uthman removed Abu Musa al-Ash'ari and gave the governorship to his maternal cousin 'Abdallah ibn 'Amir. In every case 'Uthman removed those who were early Companions and who had played important roles in the conquests of Iraq and Egypt. In contrast, 'Abdallah ibn Sa'd had apostatized and then repented, while al-Walid ibn 'Uqba and Sa'id ibn al-'As had only con- verted after the fall of Mecca to Muhammad. Both their fathers died as pagans fighting against Muhammad at the Battle of Badr.

These appointments could be justified based on the men's mili- tary ability, but their appointment was cast in a sinister light because 'Uthman appointed family members to other important posts without any apparent justification. 'Uthman not only tried to give his cousin, Marwan ibn al-Hakam, a disproportionate part of the booty from the Ifriqiya campaign, he also gave him responsibility for collecting the alms tax there. He put Marwan's brother, al-Harith, in charge of the market in Medina. Al-Harith stood accused of taking more in taxes from those in the market than was prescribed, and he provoked outrage when he took advantage of his position to buy up imported goods and then sell them at a large profit. 'Uthman ignored demands for his removal and instead gave him a gift of camels which had been collected as part of the alms-tax and brought to Medina. Likewise, Marwan used his relation- ship with 'Uthman to unfair advantage in the market. The promotion of Quraysh from Mecca with dubious credentials to have control over parts of Medina turned some of the *Ansar* against 'Uthman. Marwan and al-Harith's father, al-Hakam ibn Abi al-'As ibn Umayya, had been one of the strongest opponents to Muhammad and Muhammad had ban- ished him from Medina. When 'Uthman became caliph, he brought him back and gave him an estate that had been held as endowment by the government, presumably for the common welfare. As a family that had actively opposed Muhammad, it was particularly galling that these were now the ones "taking the money of the Muslims" and unjustly benefitting from their position and relationship with 'Uthman.

'Uthman not only appointed members of the old tribal elite to key government posts, he sought to strengthen the relationships through marriage and money. 'Uthman married his daughters to those within the old elite rather than the new Islamic elite, which suggests he thought true prestige and power resided there and that he wanted to solidify his family's position in that elite. Moreover, by some accounts, when 'Uthman married off his daughters to his various government appointees, he paid for their dowry and helped them build or enlarge their houses with money from the public treasury—treating it as his personal property. 'Uthman's abuse of the public treasury was a recurring complaint. The son of 'Uthman's business partner from before Islam wrote to 'Uthman asking him to have Ibn 'Amir, the governor in Basra, lend him 100,000 dirhams. 'Uthman went one better, he gave him the money out of the treasury as a "gift of kinship." When 'Uthman told his treasurer in Medina to bestow large financial gifts on some men, the treasurer refused to pay thinking it too exorbitant and unwarranted. 'Uthman told him that he worked for 'Uthman and to do as he was told. At this the treasurer replied that he worked for the Muslims not 'Uthman and resigned, hanging the keys to the treasury on the raised pulpit in the mosque.

Key Companions confronted 'Uthman on his appointments and failure to reign in his family members. They reminded him that 'Umar had warned him not to favor his family; 'Uthman ignored them. When Companions pointed out to 'Uthman that Abu Bakr and 'Umar had deliberately chosen not to favor their family, 'Uthman replied that it was their choice how to treat their relatives and he was making a different choice. By this 'Uthman may have been claiming for himself a right of the Prophet Muhammad to take one-fifth of booty in land and moveable goods for his own family. Abu Bakr and 'Umar had not claimed this right for their own families and had even stopped the distribution to Muhammad's family after his death. One can imagine the uncertainty at the time, especially with discretionary and surplus money, as to what honors and privileges should be accorded to the caliph. 'Uthman may just have been generous—something for which he was praised during Muhammad's life. Nevertheless, when warned, 'Uthman replied that God had given him authority and so he could do what he liked with it. The combined complaints around appointing family members and misusing money and resources that were supposed to be administered by the caliph for the welfare of all Muslims was perhaps the most significant and recurring complaint against 'Uthman. It threatened the newly achieved status and prosperity of early converts and fighters and abandoned Islamic precedent in the process. On the other hand, there was no precedent for what to do with annual revenue rather than the booty from war. Nor was there agreement on what should be done with a surplus, once stipends had been paid. 'Uthman used the discretion and influence he had to keep the prominent tribes loyal while seemingly indifferent to everyone else. 'Uthman failed to instill love, loyalty, or fear into community leaders.

The garrison city of Kufa in central Iraq was one of the centers of opposition to 'Uthman. Many of our sources are from there and the detail is especially rich and the problems particularly egregious. While governor in Kufa, al-Walid ibn 'Uqba was accused of consorting with a sorcerer and cavorting with a Christian. He allowed the latter to enter the mosque and provided him with wine and pork. Al-Walid's own drinking got so out of hand that on at least one occasion he led the communal prayers drunk, so drunk in fact that he botched the prayer, swayed in the pulpit, and vomited all over it. When the people complained about this 'Uthman did nothing. Eventually, two men snuck into al-Walid's residence when he was sleeping, slipped his signet ring off his finger and sent it to 'Uthman claiming they were able to remove it without al-Walid knowing because he had passed out, drunk. 'Uthman's initial response was to condemn not al-Walid, but his accusers. It was only when numerous Companions, especially 'Ali, confronted 'Uthman in protest and insisted that he carry out the Quranically prescribed punishment for drinking that 'Uthman ordered al-Walid brought to Medina and had him flogged. He removed al-Walid as governor and appointed Sa'id ibn al-'As in his place.

The situation in Kufa went from bad to worse under Sa'id ibn al-'As. When Sa'id arrived in Kufa he met with distinguished citizens of the town, but quickly insulted them when he described the fertile lands of Iraq, the *sawad*, as a "garden that belongs to Quraysh." This refers to 'Uthman's policy of allowing the Medinan tribes that had not participated in the conquest of Iraq to move there and granting them a portion of the state lands. Iraq was conquered by tribes from Yemen and eastern Arabia; the latter had rebelled against Abu Bakr and Qurayshi control during the *Ridda* Wars. They were rehabilitated by their participation in the Conquests, but their reaction to 'Uthman's governors and policies suggests they were still anxious about Qurayshi hegemony. They claimed Iraqi land and revenue for themselves as they had won it "with their own spears." Some, led by al-Nakha'i al-Ashtar, began to agitate for Sa'id's removal. As the unrest in Kufa grew, Sa'id wrote to 'Uthman stating he could not keep control of al-Ashtar and his friends. 'Uthman ordered them to be exiled to Syria.

Revenue

Complaints against 'Uthman were particularly fierce in Kufa because of how he changed the allocation of land in the fertile area between the Tigris and Euphrates. Previously, after a conquest, moveable goods and some lands were distributed among tribal warriors proportionally based on their precedence in conversion to Islam and role in the campaign. How lands were distributed depended as well on the terms of surrender. In many cases local people retained their land and property but paid tribute and tax, either because the Arab tribesmen did not want to farm it or, because if kept in common, the revenue was for the good of the entire community. The fertile lands around Kufa had belonged to the Sassanid nobility; they were killed, or fled, in the course of the conquests and so the land was left ownerless. These lands had not been distributed among the tribesmen, but held by the state as communal property for the benefit of the local garrison town. 'Uthman started giving this land to prominent Qurayshi leaders from Mecca. This provoked an outcry from the tribes already in Kufa. They resented sharing revenue with those who had not conquered Iraq and feared falling under Qurayshi hegemony. The new policy thus produced tension between different tribal groups, between "old-timers" and "newcomers." A loss of money and status, which could be framed as reverting to a pre-Islamic order, galvanized complaints against 'Uthman.

Kufa and other garrison cities like Fustat in Egypt also had to absorb a second wave of tribesmen from Mecca and Medina who came as reinforcements for the campaign in North Africa and northern Iran. But there was not permanent Arab settlement in those areas at that time and so the number of people from different tribes in both cities increased. This meant that those who had not participated in the conquests of Iraq and Egypt were now requiring support from the revenue generated by the province. As we saw in the previous chapter, 'Uthman's removal of 'Amr ibn al-'As from command of Egypt and the allocation of booty from the campaign in Ifriqiya were not well received by the Arabian forces there. They also complained, as in Kufa, that the revenue (and grain) from Egypt which had gone to the tribes who had conquered and settled in Egypt was now going to the Medinan. Ibn Abi Sarh, 'Uthman's new governor, was acting as 'Uthman's agent, securing the resources of Egypt for Medina, whereas 'Amr ibn al-'As had prioritized the interests of his own men. By the time of the Battle of the Masts in 655 Muhammad ibn Hudhayfa and Muhammad ibn Abi Bakr were openly criticizing Ibn Abi Sarh and 'Uthman and calling for their removal.

When those complaining against 'Uthman and his governors in Kufa as well as Basra got to be too much, 'Uthman ordered them into exile in Syria. Their complaints seemingly would not destabilize Syria as well and perhaps Mu'awiya would be able to rehabilitate them. Accounts differ as to what happened when they arrived in Syria. In one version Mu'awiya was able to adequately defend 'Uthman and the seniority of Quraysh, and even if not entirely convinced they remained silent so that Mu'awiya allowed them to return to Kufa. Alternatively, they remained obstinate and resolute in their opposition and Mu'awiya sent them on to his commander in Hims who subdued them not through argument but further exile, this time to the Taurus mountains on the Byzantine frontier.

Syria is the one province from which we hear of no disaffection with 'Uthman, his officials, or his policies. This is likely due to several factors. Mu'awiya was a particularly astute leader. 'Uthman had granted him the authority to appoint his sub-governors and he created a pyramid of loyal deputies throughout Greater Syria. More so than in Iraq or Egypt, Quraysh tribesmen had been a part of the initial campaigns of conquest. Nor does it appear that significant numbers of tribesmen moved to the province from Arabia in subsequent years. This was because Mu'awiya developed good relations with the Arab Christian tribes in Greater Syria, especially the Kalb and Tanukh. Mu'awiya, his most trusted general, Habib ibn Maslama, and 'Uthman all married women from the Kalb tribe. While this was not held against 'Uthman in the sources, at the time it may have been seen as a further example of 'Uthman and the Umayyads prioritizing those with power and influence within the old tribal system rather than Islam. These tribes may have had uneasy relations with the Byzantine townspeople of Syria and Palestine, but they were at least integrated into local political and economic life. Mu'awiya's ability to maintain stability in Syria-Palestine with the Christian population while continuing *jihad* against the Byzantines was no small feat. These tribes became the bulk of Mu'awiya's fighting men, and their strength and loyalty would prove decisive when Mu'awiya challenged 'Ali for the caliphate in the civil war that followed 'Uthman's murder.

Mu'awiya's leadership provides an instructive contrast with 'Uthman's and this may be what the early authors intended. It is not difficult to defend 'Uthman's apparent push for greater integration and "central" control and belief that the men of Umayya were best placed to achieve this. But 'Uthman did not have the mechanisms of surveillance or army to enforce it. We also do not have a record of back and forth correspondence and numerous directives as we do for the second caliph, 'Umar. 'Uthman comes across as taking more into his hands in Medina, while having a very hands-off approach to the provinces. It is hard to defend how 'Uthman went about asserting this control. He appears to have made no effort to assuage the fears coming from the tribesmen who had conquered Iraq and Egypt. He alienated powerful men like 'Amr ibn al-'As without compensation. He failed to earn the allegiance of other tribes and showed no interest in even co-opting rival forces. In contrast, Mu'awiya worked hard to keep all tribes loyal or under tight supervision. It did not help that 'Uthman was an acknowledged coward who had fled from battle and had no known experience of fighting. Perhaps his lack of experience in this area explains why he failed to understand the point of view of the tribesmen and why they wanted those who had fought with them to lead them.

Religion

During the annual pilgrimage to Mecca in 649 'Uthman knelt four times in prayer rather than the prescribed two. As the communal prayer leader this caused great consternation. 'Abd al-Rahman ibn 'Awf, who had elected 'Uthman in the *shura* council, confronted 'Uthman for changing the precedent of Muhammad, Abu Bakr, and 'Umar. 'Uthman defended himself by stating that while one kneels two times when traveling, including for the pilgrimage, the requirement is to kneel four times when at home. 'Uthman then pointed out that he was connected to a clan in Mecca, had taken his wife there to visit, and had property nearby at which he sometimes stayed after the pilgrimage. So, Mecca was in effect "home." But 'Abd al-Rahman rejected this, it did not constitute a permanent residence and 'Uthman was deviating from revelation and precedent and thus tampering with Islam. 'Uthman defended his actions as his own interpretation of Muhammad's instructions.

Another serious accusation leveled against 'Uthman was that he "burned the Qur'an." This refers to 'Uthman's decision to establish a single, authoritative text of the Qur'an and to destroy the variant versions circulating in the empire. What brought 'Uthman to this controversial act? Was it really controversial at the time or were his critics looking for things to hold against him? The narrative of events accepted within the Muslim world is as follows. During Muhammad's lifetime his revelations were written down on bones, palm leaves, potsherds, or whatever was available. But as an oral society—Qur'an after all means "recitation"—they were memorized and preserved primarily in "men's hearts." This was sufficient and even preferable while Muhammad was alive; he occasionally made amendments and clarifications in light of subsequent revelations. However, two years after Muhammad's death, at the Battle of Yamama, many of the memorizers of the Qur'an were killed. Worried that portions of the Qur'an would be lost, the caliph, Abu Bakr, ordered that the Qur'an be collected. He had 'Umar ibn al-Khattab and one of Muhammad's secretaries, Zayd ibn Thabit, gather together all the written fragments as well as memorized portions that could be confirmed by two witnesses. These were written down but not put into a single, organized volume, nor distributed to the community. Instead they were safely guarded by 'Umar during his caliphate and upon his death by his daughter, Hafsa. Different recensions and written fragments continued to circulate. As the empire expanded, variant versions and pronunciations were endorsed in the different garrison towns.

During 'Uthman's reign the different readings of the Qur'an used in the provincial garrison cities became a source of partisanship. The story is that in the year 651 armies from Syria and Iraq took part in a joint campaign in Azerbaijan and Armenia. Disputes broke out among them about the correct reading of the Qur'an, with the armies from Basra, Kufa, Homs, and Damascus each standing by their own version. Some of the commanders were greatly alarmed by this and reported it to 'Uthman, urging him to take action so that the Muslims did not become divided like the Christians and Jews. 'Uthman responded by establishing a committee in Medina, headed by Zayd ibn Thabit, whose responsibility was to produce a single, authoritative copy of the Qur'an based on the compilation held by Hafsa and with reference to other oral and written portions in circulation. If there was any discrepancy or disagreement over language or pronunciation among the committee members, they were to defer to the dialect spoken by Muhammad's tribe of Quraysh. This standard text was then copied and sent to the provincial capitals and 'Uthman ordered all variant versions to be burned.

It should be noted that at this time Arabic was still a primitive script. Vowels were not identified and even some consonants were indistinguishable from each other. The written text was a mnemonic device. Marks for vowels and dots to distinguish between similar consonants took several more centuries to develop. Nevertheless, the 'Uthmanic Qur'an established the content and order of the verses and chapters in the Qur'an. And by establishing a single, written version it greatly restricted possible variations. It also established the pronunciation to be used when in subsequent centuries the script developed to distinguish between similar consonants and to include vowel markers. The Qur'an of today is regarded by Muslims to be the heir of 'Uthman's Quranic codex. Yet initially 'Uthman was criticized rather than lauded for his efforts to unify and codify the Qur'an. For 'Uthman's critics it was government overreach by a controversial caliph into the devotional life of believers, another example of 'Uthman's abuse of power. Furthermore, 'Uthman's "destruction" of the Qur'an was developed by some Shi'is who claimed that in the process passages that referred to 'Ali, and especially to Muhammad's appointment of 'Ali as his successor, were intentionally burned. To accuse 'Uthman and the revered Companions on the committee of destroying the Qur'an in order to secure political power is perhaps the most serious charge that could be leveled against them.

Response

It was not the centralizing policies alone or 'Uthman's personal interpretations that turned people against 'Uthman; it was how he responded to those who tried to counsel or confront him that shifts perceptions of 'Uthman from an incompetent ruler to a corrupt and tyrannical one. When prominent Companions, like 'A'isha or 'Ali, confronted 'Uthman, he ignored them. When those from lowly tribal backgrounds dared to do so, he had them beaten. This angered the pious, the tribes of the beaten men, and the Qurayshi clans who sponsored them. The sources focus on 'Uthman's treatment of three men who fall into this category: 'Abdallah ibn Mas'ud, 'Ammar ibn Yasir, and Abu Dharr al-Ghifari. In Medina 'Ammar ibn Yasir and Ibn Mas'ud, both early converts, spoke out against 'Uthman's abuse of the treasury and religious innovations. 'Uthman had them both beaten. 'A'isha and others found this outrageous and the murmurings against 'Uthman increased. Abu Dharr al-Ghifari was a highly regarded ascetic who criticized Mu'awiya and 'Uthman for the growing decadence and neglect of the poor and needy. 'Uthman responded by exiling Abu Dharr to live with Bedouin in the desert. 'Uthman's harsh treatment of these men, added to his religious innovations, meant that prominent Companions and even elements within Quraysh were frustrated with him. Consider 'Abd al-Rahman ibn 'Awf who had played the decisive role in 'Uthman's election. He had had a falling-out with 'Uthman because of 'Uthman's abusive policies to the point that he refused to speak to 'Uthman and when he fell ill willed that 'Uthman not be allowed to pray over him when he died. Thus, after ten years as leader of the Community, 'Uthman had managed to alienate the tribes in the garrison cities, the *Ansar* in Medina, some of the Quraysh, and prominent Companions.

While 'Uthman was indifferent to the complaints and warnings coming from key Companions, in 654 he called his governors to meet with him in Medina, probably during the pilgrimage to Mecca, and confer about how best to respond to the growing discontent in the provinces. Mu'awiya put the responsibility on the governors and said that they had to administer their regions with care. 'Abdallah ibn 'Amir from Basra urged sending the dissidents on *jihad* so that they would be too busy to speak out against 'Uthman. Meanwhile, 'Abdallah ibn Sa'd from Egypt asserted that while those agitating against 'Uthman and his governors might have some (legitimate) grievances, they were also greedy. He predicted that if 'Uthman would give them a greater share of the empire's new wealth they would stop complaining. Sa'id ibn al-'As from Kufa argued that if 'Uthman killed the leaders of the opposition in each province, their followers would split into factions and be unable to unify or organize any opposition against him. 'Uthman agreed that while those ends were desirable the means were unacceptable. 'Uthman sent his governors back to the provinces urging them to assert their authority and to keep the people busy with the conquests. Rather than being more generous 'Uthman decided to cut the people's stipends as punishment and in order to have more leverage over them. It is impossible to know whether the foregoing was the kind of advice 'Uthman actually received. What is recorded seems designed to fit the reputations associated with each character. What is certain is that the situation deteriorated.

REBELLION

The growing dissatisfaction in the garrison towns came to a head in the year 655 when criticism turned to coordinated confrontations.

Companions of the Prophet in Medina wrote to the Companions in the provinces complaining about the abuses of 'Uthman's governors and that he had abandoned the precedent of Muhammad, Abu Bakr, and 'Umar. They called for others to join them in Medina to wage *jihad* against 'Uthman. They argued that while the Muslims had been fighting in the path of God on the frontier, 'Uthman was corrupting and abandoning Islam at home. By presenting 'Uthman's appointments and policies as an attack on Islam, disgruntled parties sought to broaden their base of support. When, however, these Companions confronted 'Uthman he defended himself on the basis that God had allowed him to be chosen caliph; it followed that God endorsed his policies, so he proposed no changes.

The following year, in 656, delegations from Egypt, Iraq, and Basra agreed to meet in Medina during the pilgrimage and confront 'Uthman together. This initiative was led by those from Egypt. Earlier 'Uthman had sent 'Ammar ibn Yasir to Egypt to quell the complaints there, but 'Ammar had stirred up the Egyptians against 'Uthman instead. There are different versions of what happened next. In one 'Uthman refused to meet with the delegations, either out of fear or arrogance, and instead asked others to go and speak with them on his behalf, including 'Ali. If 'Ali went, he went reluctantly, pointing out that 'Uthman had ignored all his earlier advice. 'Uthman promised that this time he would abide by whatever agreement 'Ali came to with the band of protestors. The Egyptians, backed by the others, criticized 'Uthman's government appointments and demanded that 'Uthman remove Ibn Abi Sarh and appoint Muhammad ibn Abi Bakr as governor in Egypt instead and stop giving Egyptian money to the Medinese. 'Ali accepted their demands and signed a covenant with them to that effect. In an alternative version, 'Uthman met with the group directly and they confronted him with his various abuses. They accused him of banishing men of piety and nobility and taking from the public treasury for his personal use. 'Uthman wept and repented and promised to do what they asked of him. In both versions the key point appears to be that 'Uthman promised to make changes in Egypt. Why now? It could be that 'Uthman finally understood the level of discontent in the provinces. Alternatively, it may have been a ruse to get them to leave Medina and give him time to launch a counteroffensive. Some accounts claim when 'Uthman repented to the Egyptian delegation, Marwan ibn al-Hakam came to 'Uthman and reprimanded him, arguing that his public repentance was a sign of weakness. He argued: "To persist in an error for which you must seek God's forgiveness is better than to repent because you are afraid." 'Uthman agreed and asked Marwan to speak to the people. Marwan did not so much speak to the people as threaten them. He accused them of being looters, intent on seizing power and possessions, and warned that they would not be allowed to get away with it. At that the group from Egypt (and Iraq) departed. When word reached 'Ali that 'Uthman had listened to Marwan and threatened the Egyptian delegation after 'Ali had made a covenant with them, he washed his hands of 'Uthman and retreated into his house, swearing to have nothing more to do with him.

On their journey home the Egyptian delegation came across a messenger who was one of 'Uthman's servants, riding 'Uthman's camel, and when they searched the messenger, they found hidden in a water bag a message that bore 'Uthman's seal. The message was to 'Uthman's governor in Egypt, 'Abdallah ibn Abi Sarh, ordering him, upon the group's arrival in Egypt, to crucify them or amputate their hands and feet and "let them soak in their blood until they die." The band returned to Medina, confronted 'Uthman, and laid siege to him in his house. The groups from Kufa and Basra joined them. Although 'Uthman denied any knowledge of the letter they demanded that he step down or they would fight and kill him. Some modern scholars speculate that the letter to the Egyptians was a detail manufactured later to pin the final climax of the rebellion on this single incident and then to claim that 'Uthman did not know about the letter. It can also seem odd, in light of all the other abuses held against 'Uthman, that so much should be pinned on this letter. But it did mark an important departure in policy; whereas others had been exiled or beaten this letter was the first time that killing dissidents was contemplated.

'Uthman was held directly or indirectly responsible for the letter, despite his vociferous and repeated denials of any knowledge of it. Either he wrote it or he had lost control of his administration and household if it could be written without his knowledge. In either case he had to go. 'Uthman offered to repent and desist from the behavior they hated, but the people pointed out that it was too late and they had no reason to believe him after he had repented in the past and then continued with the same behavior. 'Uthman, fearing for his life, sought the counsel of his advisors and family members who told him to send for 'Ali and have him negotiate with the besiegers on 'Uthman's behalf. 'Uthman initially hesitated because he knew this time he would have to keep his promises. Marwan, however, told him simply to use negotiations with 'Ali as a stalling tactic. When 'Ali arrived, he pointed out to 'Uthman that the people wanted justice more than his death. 'Uthman asked for three days to address their grievances, 'Ali presented this to the besiegers, another covenant was signed, and they withdrew. 'Uthman used the time to gather weapons and prepare for war. He wrote to Mu'awiya in Syria and 'Abdallah ibn 'Amir in Basra urging them to hurry to Medina with reinforcements in order to defend him and to fight the rebels. Only when the three days had passed and 'Uthman had neither removed the contentious governors nor made any other changes did the people revolt in earnest and surround him in his house.

'Uthman was besieged for forty days during which time the people of Medina also turned on 'Uthman and prominent Companions abandoned him or turned against him. During the first twenty or thirty days 'Uthman still was able to access the mosque and led the people in prayer. As described above, on at least one occasion when he did so he was shouted down by 'Amr ibn al-'As who had harbored resentment against 'Uthman since his removal from the governorship of Egypt. Likewise, Jahjah al-Ghifari, Abu Dharr's kinsman, seized the Prophet's staff from 'Uthman's hand and broke it over his knee. There are also reports of the congregation throwing stones at 'Uthman and knocking him off the pulpit so that he fell to the ground unconscious and had to be carried into his home by family members. Meanwhile 'A'isha was stirring up the crowds against 'Uthman, but then she abandoned Medina to make the pilgrimage to Mecca. She encouraged 'Abdallah ibn 'Abbas, who was leading the pilgrimage that year in 'Uthman's place, to delay the pilgrims' return to Medina. The implication is that this is why there were not more men in Medina to defend 'Uthman.

At the same time, Talha, and to a lesser degree al-Zubayr, from the *shura* council, were leading calls for 'Uthman's removal. Towards the end of the siege Talha blocked water from getting to 'Uthman and those with him in his house. When 'Ali heard of this he insisted that they be given water.

REGICIDE

Efforts to relate the specific events surrounding the murder of 'Uthman are impossibly entangled in the larger crisis of killing a Companion and killing a caliph. Accordingly, there are multiple versions of the final assault that vilify and honor different individuals and to varying degrees contrast 'Uthman's piety with the attacker's aggression. In one version, Muhammad ibn Abi Bakr and three companions scaled the walls of 'Uthman's house and broke into 'Uthman's room, where they found him with his wife, Na'ila, reading the Qur'an. 'Uthman put the Qur'an on his lap and promised to abide by what was in it and repented of all they hated. Ibn Abi Bakr replied, however, "What! Now! When previously you have been obstinate and among the mischief makers?" Muhammad ibn Abi Bakr grabbed 'Uthman's beard and insulted him and 'Uthman cried out to God for help. 'Uthman told him his father, the first caliph, Abu Bakr, would never have done this to which Muhammad replied that had his father witnessed 'Uthman's behavior he would have denounced him. Then Muhammad and those with him stabbed 'Uthman repeatedly in the head and neck and 'Uthman's blood flowed on to the Quranic verse: "God will suffice you over them. He is the all-hearing and all-knowing" (Q 2:137). That Muhammad ibn Abi Bakr, the son of a prominent Companion and the first caliph, would kill another prominent Companion and caliph was hard to accept. Alternative versions describe Muhammad entering 'Uthman's room, but when he saw 'Uthman praying and reading the Qur'an, Muhammad was overcome by 'Uthman's piety and withdrew so that it was other marginal figures who actually assaulted 'Uthman.

One version of events describes a battle at the house between 'Uthman's defenders and the besiegers. In this version, one of the defenders, Marwan's servant, either threw down a stone or shot an arrow that killed one of the besiegers, and this is what provoked them into a final assault on the house. News of the forces coming from Syria and Basra also spurred the besiegers on. As the battle unfolded 'Uthman was strongly defended by Marwan and the sons of other Companions, including the sons of 'Ali ibn Abi Talib and al-Zubayr. Eventually the besiegers set the door to 'Uthman's house ablaze, and after a brief fight at the door, 'Uthman's defenders fled. 'Uthman was alone in his room with his wife reading the Qur'an when the besiegers broke in and stabbed him to death.

Even 'Uthman's burial was controversial and contested. According to some his body was left in the house for a day or possibly three days. His wives and those who had been in the house were afraid to bury him during the day for fear that his corpse would be attacked by angry mobs still roaming the streets. Accordingly, he was buried at night or twilight. Even so, the small assembly that accompanied his body was pelted with stones. None of 'Uthman's Umayyad kinsmen and no Companions were in the company. There were also protests that 'Uthman not be buried in the main cemetery as his behavior was unbefitting a Companion of the Prophet. Instead he was buried in a compound set apart for the Jews, although eventually others were buried around the area and it became incorporated into the main Muslim cemetery. The difficulty in burying 'Uthman shows the passions that continued to swirl around Medina and the violence that had been unleashed. In the chaos it was not clear what would or should happen next.

AFTERMATH

Who should succeed 'Uthman as Commander of the (not so faithful) Faithful? The rebels, supported by the *Ansar* of Medina, sought out 'Ali ibn Abi Talib and offered him the oath of loyalty. 'Ali was in an impossible position. He had been waiting for this moment possibly since Muhammad's death, but the circumstances and personages that finally were offering it to him undermined his legitimacy from the start. Nevertheless, 'Ali accepted and other Companions swore allegiance to him. 'A'isha, Talha and al-Zubayr initially gave 'Ali the oath of allegiance but then retracted. 'A'isha had a long-standing grudge against 'Ali. Once when she was young and had been traveling with an expeditionary force she had become separated from the group; she was found by a handsome young man who brought her to Medina. At that point rumors of impropriety, or even immorality, began to fly. Some, especially 'Ali, urged Muhammad to divorce her. 'A'isha was only spared because Muhammad received a revelation (Q 24:4–9) exonerating her. At the same time 'A'isha's kinsman, Talha ibn 'Ubaydallah, and the Prophet's cousin, al-Zubayr ibn al-'Awwam, may have realized 'Ali was actually in a weak position needing as he did to punish 'Uthman's killers but aware that that would cause a revolt among his supporters. In light of the circumstances they may have concluded that they had a chance of becoming the next caliph, and they had just as much right as 'Ali based on their early and vigorous support of Muhammad. The three exploited 'Ali's weakness and demanded he punish 'Uthman's killers as proof of his authority. This was purely opportunistic since the three had either abandoned 'Uthman to his fate or actively goaded on the crowds against 'Uthman. The three withdrew to Basra and gathered together an army to oppose 'Ali. 'Ali followed them to Iraq and marshalled his supporters in Kufa. The two armies met at the Battle of the Camel. 'Ali won the battle but everyone lost the war as the first generation of Muslims turned on each other in armed combat. Both Talha and al-Zubayr were killed; 'A'isha was sent back to Medina in disgrace where she lived out her days removed from public affairs.

Mu'awiya, meanwhile, had been en route to Medina when he received word of 'Uthman's death, returned to Syria to wait and see how things would develop. He did not swear allegiance to 'Ali, but rather demanded justice for 'Uthman. He adopted a wait and see attitude as the power struggle between those with impeccable "Companion" credentials played itself out. As 'Uthman's cousin it was appropriate that he led the Umayyad demand for justice for 'Uthman's murder. He used this to his own advantage. He did not participate in the Battle of the Camel, but even when 'Ali emerged as the victor

Mu'awiya refused to recognize him as caliph. Instead he demanded 'Ali punish 'Uthman's killers, but 'Ali was more indebted to them and to the tribes in Kufa than before. 'Ali and Mu'awiya and their respective armies met at the Battle of Siffin in Syria in 657. The battle was violent but inconclusive and once again 'Ali's legitimacy was compromised. His supporters initially demanded he submit to arbitration and then later regretted it and blamed 'Ali for doing so. As 'Ali's coalition of supporters fragmented and weakened Mu'awiya's solidified and strengthened. In 660 in Jerusalem Mu'awiya declared himself *Amir al-Mu'minin*, Commander of the Believers. We will never know whether 'Ali would have been able to fight back; he was assassinated in 661 by one of his own disgruntled former supporters.

If 'Uthman had been trying to secure the position of the Qurayshi elite and the Umayyads in the new Islamic order then he succeeded. However, if 'Uthman had been trying to strengthen the administrative and economic bonds of the new Arab Islamic community, then his legacy is more mixed. The Umayyads ruled from Damascus for nearly a hundred years. Even when they were overthrown by the 'Abbasids, a survivor from the royal house, 'Abd al-Rahman I, made his way to Arab controlled Spain and established an Umayyad rule there, first as princes of different city-states until his descendant, 'Abd al-Rahman III declared himself caliph in 929. The Umayyad Caliphate of the West lasted for another hundred years. Mu'awiya insisted the different provinces submit to his authority, but he allowed considerable regional autonomy. Mu'awiya appointed 'Amr ibn al-'As governor of Egypt. They had clearly come to an understanding early on in which Mu'awiya promised to restore 'Umar's position in Egypt in exchange for his support against 'Ali. Mu'awiya had to work a lot harder to subdue Iraq, especially Kufa, and he appointed governors there who demanded loyalty to Mu'awiya but treated the Arabian tribesmen with respect. Mu'awiya did a better job of wielding a stick of violence and the carrot of shared interests. Mu'awiya's own distinguished career in the battles of conquest—he continued to oversee the campaigns in Anatolia and the Mediterranean—earned him the respect of tribal chiefs and fighting men. Also, unlike 'Uthman, Mu'awiya promoted talent wherever he found it and was not accused of promoting the

Umayyads over all others. Finally, while a small percentage of revenue was sent to Mu'awiya in Damascus, the vast majority stayed in the provinces. Mu'awiya was a more astute leader, but he also had an army loyal to himself that enabled him to threaten Iraq into submission. An army was something 'Uthman did not have or at least he did not consider sending troops from one garrison to attack those of another. 'Uthman receives no credit for this.

Mu'awiya appointed his son to succeed him as caliph. Mu'awiya's introduction of hereditary rule was held against him to such a strong degree that despite the successes of his rule he is not considered one of the Rightly Guided (Rashidun) Caliphs. But this is unfair. The two rebellions against his son Yazid were led by Ali's son, Husayn, and al-Zubayr's son, 'Abdallah. Like 'Uthman, Mu'awiya was in an impossible situation that led once again to civil war, the Second Fitna (680–692). 'Abdallah ibn al-Zubayr declared himself caliph and managed to outlive Yazid and Marwan ibn al-Hakam who became caliph after al-Yazid. At one point 'Abdallah controlled more territory than Marwan's son, the caliph 'Abd al-Malik; nevertheless, 'Abd al-Malik's forces eventually killed 'Abdallah in Mecca and his movement died with him. In contrast, Husayn ibn 'Ali was killed by Yazid's forces almost immediately, in the horrible massacre at Karbala in Iraq in 680. But the movement that supported him lived on in opposition to the Marwanid line of the Umayyad Caliphate, contributing to its overthrow by the 'Abbasids in 750, and evolving into Shi'i Islam.

For the Umayyads 'Uthman became a source of political legitimacy rather than a political liability. Mu'awiya astutely leveraged the demand for vengeance for 'Uthman into a position in which he could rival 'Ali's claim to the caliphate. The Umayyads built an ideology of political legitimacy not on sabiqa, but on the glory of Quraysh. God had honored Quraysh when He chose Muhammad to be His messenger. Through Muhammad and therefore through Quraysh, all the Arabs had been blessed. 'Uthman in death regained the significance that had gotten him elected leader in the first place. The Umayyad rulers emphasized their linkages to 'Uthman, his status as a member of Quraysh and Muhammad's inner circle who was chosen by other Companions of the Prophet to lead the Community.

CONCLUSION

In the historical record 'Uthman stands accused of lavishing wealth on his family, appointing family members to key government posts who then abused their power, altering the communal prayer, changing how taxes were collected and revenue and land distributed, and treating the public treasury as his personal purse. He was indifferent to the growing resentment from injured parties and alienated groups, culminating in acts of tyrannical violence as 'Uthman punished any and all who tried to warn or confront him. However, there is also a sense that disgruntled elements were looking for things to hold against 'Uthman and that too many others had lost faith in 'Uthman. Although 'Uthman was an early convert and close companion of Muhammad he was an incompetent ruler if not a corrupt one. Perhaps 'Uthman miscalculated people's response to his policies because he genuinely could not imagine that Muslims would turn on each other. In a rapidly expanding empire 'Uthman was likely out of touch, unable to grasp the level of frustration in the provinces. As someone who had privilege and wealth before and after the rise of Islam, 'Uthman failed to understand how his policies appeared to threaten new-found privilege based on *sabiqa* and *jihad*. 'Uthman both overestimated and underestimated the strength of the new order. Perhaps also he was deceived by 'Umar's success and failed to appreciate the vigilance and good fortune that undergirded it. 'Uthman struggled to translate tribal and Islamic precedent into his rapidly changing milieu. In turn chroniclers struggled to balance 'Uthman's failings with the challenges of changing circumstances and unintended consequences. But they had to do more than explain the rebellion against 'Uthman; they had to make meaning out of the murder of a Companion of the Prophet and regicide.

The centrality and elevation of the Companions of the Prophet in the context of *hadith* studies and Sunni–Shi'i debates had a profound impact on portrayals of 'Uthman. 'Uthman the individual had to be reconciled with 'Uthman the Companion. In accounts of the rebellion and regicide historians were also wrestling with 'Uthman as a paradigmatic caliph. To write about the rights and wrongs of overthrowing 'Uthman was, essentially, to debate doing so to any ruler.

6

CONSEQUENCES

INTRODUCTION

Sunni scholars developed two rhetorical strategies to respond to the challenge of 'Uthman. One was to vindicate 'Uthman and the Companions by portraying him as a pious ruler who died a martyr. The second was to leave 'Uthman as a less than ideal caliph, but to assert the primacy of the unity of the community even in the face of injustice and tyranny. The first focuses on 'Uthman as a paradigmatic Companion. Muhammad's praise of 'Uthman's generosity and declaration that 'Uthman will die a martyr are bolstered by a narrative of 'Uthman's caliphate that portrays him as a righteous ruler who died a violent death because of his devotion to Muhammad and the Qur'an. The second strategy treats 'Uthman as a paradigmatic caliph. Rather than defending 'Uthman it focuses on condemning his killers because they "unsheathed the sword of *fitna*" upon the community. The first approach is found in *fada'il* and polemical works while the second is found in early chronicles. Al-Tabari (d. 923) interweaves both and therefore so do the later chroniclers who rely on him for the early Islamic period. Having included the criticisms leveled against 'Uthman that provoked the rebellion, chroniclers then use confrontations between 'Uthman and the rebels to debate the appropriate response to injustice. They conclude obedience to the ruler is necessary for the sake of the *umma*. In both rhetorical strategies the causes of the rebellion discussed in the previous chapter are either erased or overshadowed by its consequences. The final verdict on 'Uthman is not based on the strength of his character or the merit of his policies, but the cataclysmic consequences of his murder: the permanent rupture of the community into Sunni and Shi'i Islam, and civil war that ushered in dynastic kingship. As the first rebellion in Islamic history its consequences created the scales upon which all rebellions would be weighed.

MARTYR

Practically every treatment of 'Uthman includes and usually concludes with *hadith* in which Muhammad declares 'Uthman a martyr. As discussed in the chapter on 'Uthman's virtues as a Companion of the Prophet, *hadith* that recorded Muhammad's relationship with and assessment of a person acted as a verdict on that person. In numerous *hadith* Muhammad refers to the first three caliphs as the friend (Abu Bakr) and the two martyrs ('Umar and 'Uthman). Furthermore, in the narratives of the siege of 'Uthman sources include accounts in which 'Uthman has numerous dedicated supporters who could have defeated the assailants, but 'Uthman prevented them from fighting on his behalf. This was because he did not want to be the source of intra-Muslim violence and because he anticipated being with Muhammad in Paradise. 'Uthman informed his supporters that Muhammad had told him of the fate that was going to befall him and made him promise to patiently endure it. The impact of this *hadith* is bolstered further when at the height of the siege 'Uthman reportedly had a dream in which Muhammad appeared to him and told him he would breakfast with him that day in Paradise. (It is a part of Islamic martyrology that the martyr is immediately in Paradise with Muhammad.) It was for this reason that 'Uthman did not resist; he was joyfully anticipating his reunion with Muhammad. This not only exonerates 'Uthman, but also the Companions by showing their loyalty to 'Uthman while also explaining why they allowed 'Uthman to be killed.

But *hadith* on 'Uthman's generosity towards the community at the beginning of Muhammad's mission and 'Uthman's obedience to Muhammad at the end of his own life do not adequately address all that

'Uthman did in between while he was caliph. Built on the scaffolding provided by *hadith*, a counter-narrative of 'Uthman's caliphate was gradually and carefully crafted that refuted every accusation leveled against 'Uthman. 'Uthman appears as a righteous victim persecuted for his devotion to Muhammad, the Qur'an, and the welfare of the believers. All the Companions remained loyal to 'Uthman until the end; the growing resentment and revolt against 'Uthman came from disgruntled individuals spurred on by a heretical conspiracy movement intent on ruining 'Uthman and Islam. 'Uthman's piety in the final stages of the siege is accentuated and contrasted with the attackers' greed and violence to create a more dramatic martyr narrative.

This exercise is perhaps best captured in the history of the first *fitna* written by Sayf ibn 'Umar (d. *c*.800) that al-Tabari incorporated into his chronicle. Sayf's counter-narrative presents 'Uthman as first of all righteous and innocent by refuting all the accusations against him. Sayf does not mention the family connection in 'Uthman's appointees, but instead focuses on their abilities, virtues, and positions they held during 'Umar's caliphate. There was no inappropriate favoritism towards his family, clan, or tribe. Nor was anyone else unduly beaten or tortured.

Sayf's portrayal of the al-Walid affair in Kufa provides a good example of his approach. Rather than consulting a sorcerer, 'Uthman's governor in Kufa, al-Walid, brought in the man accused of sorcery in order to interrogate him, confirm his guilt, and determine the appropriate punishment according to the Qur'an. He was then falsely accused of consulting with the sorcerer. Likewise, Al-Walid did not abuse alcohol alone nor with a Christian companion. Instead he converted the Christian to Islam and was falsely accused of drunkenness out of malice by those he had removed from office. They snuck in while he was sleeping, took his signet ring, went to 'Uthman, and claimed they had seen him throwing up wine. Even though 'Uthman suspected the accusations were false, he ordered al-Walid brought to Medina and whipped since this was the Quranically prescribed punishment. Whereas other sources portray al-Walid as clearly guilty and 'Uthman reluctant to punish him, according to Sayf, al-Walid was innocent, but 'Uthman bowed to the will of the Companions and made a point

of following the Quranic injunction. 'Uthman urged al-Walid to suffer patiently, pointing out that if the testimony against him was false,
his accusers would suffer for it in hell. Al-Walid's personal sacrifice
for the good of the community foreshadows how Sayf will portray
'Uthman's murder as martyrdom.

This cycle of narration lays out what became the standard defense
of 'Uthman echoed in later chronicles and developed in *fada'il* and
polemical works. The variant points of discussion reflect a complex
engagement of historical anecdotes with ongoing disputes on matters
of law and religion in general. In relation to changing the number of
times 'Uthman knelt in prayer during the pilgrimage, 'Uthman did
have a residence nearby so it was right to kneel four times in prayer.
'Uthman did not give land in Iraq to Quraysh, but rather sold them
the land in exchange for their estates in Arabia. In terms of "destroying
the Qur'an," the Qur'an was "one" and he merely worked to preserve
that unity. Over time this joined praise of 'Uthman's early generosity
as one of 'Uthman's enduring contributions to the Community—one
of the few things from his caliphate for which there is genuine praise
rather than denial and deflection. While his critics claimed he brought
back al-Hakam whom the Prophet had exiled, 'Uthman reminded
them that Muhammad had pardoned al-Hakam and was intending to
bring him back from exile, but he died before he could do so. They
accused him of appointing youths, but his appointees had all proven
themselves to be able leaders. The dissidents said 'Uthman gave one-
fifth of the booty from Ifriqiya to Ibn Abi Sarh, but 'Uthman gave one-
fifth out of his own portion so it was 'Uthman and not the Muslims
who suffered. Finally, the dissidents claimed that 'Uthman loved his
kinsmen and gave them gifts from the public treasury, while 'Uthman
was merely generous towards his family; he gave to them out of his
own wealth and never from what belonged to the Muslims. Indeed, he
had given away so many of his own possessions that he had only two
camels to be used for performing the pilgrimage to Mecca.

If 'Uthman's actions and record were all proper, one wonders why
then was there a revolt against him. To answer this unsettling tension
in the accounts, Sayf, al-Tabari, and the chroniclers who followed in his
footsteps point to malicious outside intrusion into the harmony of the

community. Those who agitated against 'Uthman were disgruntled individuals who knew they did not have legitimate grievances. Their murmurings were only able to become a rebellion against 'Uthman because in places like Kufa the men of noble character and good judgment were all serving as leaders in newly conquered areas in Iran. More specifically, the key spark for the trend towards chaos is attributed to one 'Abdallah ibn Saba' who moved around the provinces trying to stir up hostility against the third caliph. The opposition takes on an added dimension of heresy in the way Ibn Saba', a Yemeni Jewish convert to Islam, referred to by the pejorative title Ibn al-Sawda (son of a black woman), preached multiple messages of schismatic belief. Ibn Saba' not only tarnished the image of 'Uthman, but undermined his legitimacy for the office of caliphate when compared to 'Ali. This would have been bad enough, but Ibn Saba' also taught that every prophet had a legatee (*wasi*) and that 'Ali was the *wasi* of Muhammad and combined this with the idea of the Prophet's return, much as in the belief in the second coming of Jesus. The overall picture of the unravelling situation therefore consisted not only of a political dispute but of a heretical doctrine at work. Sayf explains why the opposition to 'Uthman was strong in Egypt by claiming it was Ibn Saba's main base of operation and that he preached most openly there, but this also contrasted with Syria where the people reportedly drove him away in a foreshadowing of loyalty to 'Uthman and eventually Mu'awiya. Followers of Ibn Saba' then wrote back and forth to coordinate their efforts, share news of their growing strength, and exploit any dissatisfaction with 'Uthman. Ibn Saba' and the "Saba'iyya movement" was the reason why specific grievances turned into open rebellion and why calls for policy changes became calls for regime change.

When the members of the Saba'iyya movement and those they had managed to deceive in Kufa, Basra, and Fustat met in Medina to confront 'Uthman they had no legitimate grievances, only a desire to sow discord and division. Each provincial delegation wanted a different Companion to become the new caliph. The group from Basra wanted Talha, the Kufans wanted al-Zubayr, and the Egyptians wanted 'Ali. However, when they approached each of these Companions they were rebuffed. The central drift of al-Tabari's accounts juxtaposes the solidarity of the Companions with the divisiveness of the Saba'iyya. When 'Uthman went out to meet them he successfully defended his record and the delegations realized they had been deceived. As 'Uthman's critics showed contrition, the third caliph offered to make amends and to appoint over them as governor men of their own choosing. But as reconciliation was about to prevail, the Saba'iyya are shown contriving to revive the discord by planting a letter in the baggage of 'Uthman's messenger. This letter contained a command from the caliph to his governor in Egypt to punish these critics in clear violation of what 'Uthman had just promised in terms of amnesty. And the result was predictably the resurgence of heightened anger by the opposition. The stage was therefore set for an act of aggression on the caliph.

While all this was unravelling outside Medina, the caliph is portrayed as oblivious to these dangers, and immersed in a pious life. Sayf paints an image of 'Uthman in saintly passiveness, juxtaposing 'Uthman's piety and the unity of the Companions with the attackers' greed and violence. The majority of the people supported 'Uthman and opposed the besiegers, but 'Uthman insisted they not defend him. Indeed, the besiegers decided to kill 'Uthman, not only because they feared approaching reinforcements, but because they had gotten themselves into an intractable situation in which killing 'Uthman would provide a distraction so they could escape. The besiegers were the ones who first threw stones into 'Uthman's house hoping to provoke an attack by 'Uthman's defenders which would then justify the rebels' final assault on the house. The Companions did not do more to defend 'Uthman not only because 'Uthman ordered them not to, but because they did not think it would end in murder and violence—a miscalculation they later regretted. Sayf emphasizes that throughout the siege 'Uthman was reading the Qur'an until the attackers kicked it out of his hands. The attackers set the door ablaze and broke in, struck 'Uthman, but were afraid to kill him. However, 'Uthman was old and lost consciousness even as his wife and daughters were screaming, trying to defend him. Then a man named al-Tujibi, whom Sayf had earlier identified as among the Egyptian dissidents who traveled to Medina with Ibn Saba', drew his sword, plunged it into 'Uthman's chest, and then leaned on it to drive it in. 'Uthman's wife tried to shield him and her hand was severed in the process. One of the attackers cried out, "How is it that his blood is lawful and his property forbidden?" They pillaged everything, and then broke into the public treasury. The two guards threw down the keys and fled for their lives, shouting, "Flee! Flee! This is what the rebels are after." In this way Sayf makes the important point that 'Uthman's killers (and by extension his critics) were nothing more than thieves and murderers. Sayf claims 'Uthman's wife sent his bloody shirt to Mu'awiya and he waved it before his men in Syria as they demanded revenge for 'Uthman's blood.

Sayf's narrative has enduring appeal because it supports what Sunni Muslims want to believe about 'Uthman and the Companions, even though its central villain, the nefarious 'Abdallah ibn Saba', is almost certainly apocryphal. According to Sayf, 'Uthman was not abandoned by the Companions nor attacked by fellow believers; those who criticized 'Uthman were (and are) Shi'i extremists bent on the destruction of the Muslim community. Narratives about the Companions shaped Sunni and Shi'i identities and then continued to police the boundary between those two identities.

In the Sunni world, the story of 'Uthman's turbulent reign took on additional importance as a morality lesson in the need for religious consensus. It formed a central pillar in the writings of late tenth/ early eleventh-century Sunni ideologues, such as Baqillani and Abu Mansur al-Baghdadi, who set out to refute the opinions of other sects (Shi'i, Mutazila, etc.) and preached the message of reverence for all the Companions of the Prophet. Similarly, in later medieval *fada'il* works writers followed the redemptive notes in al-Tabari's history, and reconciled this with *hadith* literature moving beyond the implicit defense of 'Uthman, found in *hadith* praising 'Uthman's behavior as one of Muhammad's Companions, to an explicit defense of 'Uthman and his caliphate. Ibn 'Asakir's lengthy "biography" of 'Uthman in his *History of Damascus* relies heavily on *hadith*, largely skips over the events of 'Uthman's caliphate, and where necessary uses Sayf's version. In *The Radiant Practice of the Virtues of the Ten Promised Paradise*, 'Abdallah Muhibb al-Din al-Tabari (d. 1295) cites 'Uthman's virtues as described in *hadith*, but then goes on the offensive, listing and then

refuting the accusations leveled against 'Uthman. He does acknowledge that 'Uthman made mistakes and that there were divisions in
the community, but these divisions were created and exploited by
extremist Shi'is. He does not refer to the elusive Ibn Saba' but rather
blames the revolt against 'Uthman and any criticisms against 'Uthman
on the *Rawafid*, that is those who "reject" the legitimacy of the first
three caliphs, in other words most Shi'is.

Abu Bakr ibn al-'Arabi (d. 1148), a scholar and traditionist from
Seville, wrote *Preservation from Destruction* in which he presents a series
of historical and theological disasters that befell the Islamic community and then presents how the community was preserved from them.
He did this through refuting a particular heresy or giving different historical interpretations of an event. According to Ibn al-'Arabi, chroniclers, like those who relayed the narratives discussed in the previous
chapter, "concoct [stories] to poison weak hearts, which stories they
push into people's heads to make them despise their forefathers and
disregard religion" (Ibn al-'Arabi, 350). In his treatment of "the disas-
ter of injustices falsely attributed to 'Uthman," he presents a list of thir-
teen accusations against 'Uthman, which he labels the "stories of liars."
These include everything from 'Uthman's absence at the Battle of Badr
to "burning" the Qur'an, appointment of licentious family members
like al-Walid or those who had opposed Muhammad like Mu'awiya, to
torturing critics like 'Ammar ibn Yasir and Ibn Mas'ud. Ibn al-'Arabi
rejected most accusations as false accounts which he countered with
assertions that had become standard apologetics in Sunni ideology. But
he also relied heavily on the a priori assumption that the Companions
could not have done anything blameworthy. Accounts that portray the
Companions criticizing or opposing 'Uthman were "manufactured to
make the hearts of the Muslims boil with anger against their forefathers
in the past and the Rashidun Caliphate" (Ibn al-'Arabi, 281). Because
'Uthman did not do anything wrong during his caliphate, blame for
the siege and murder hangs on the letter to 'Uthman's Egyptian governor to kill the dissidents upon their return; but 'Uthman did not
write that letter. Ibn al-'Arabi insisted none of the Companions were
among those who attacked 'Uthman; if 'Uthman had only asked for
help, 1,000–4,000 or 20,000 or more would have come to his aid,

"but he surrendered himself to the catastrophe" (Ibn al-'Arabi, 297). Ibn al-'Arabi concluded, therefore, that if we "strain out of the matter of 'Uthman all that was unjustly and falsely attributed to him, it will be seen that 'Uthman was killed unjustly and without excuse" (Ibn al-'Arabi, 298).

'Uthman's image as martyr achieves perhaps its fullest rendition in the Andalusian Ibn Bakr al-Maliqi's (d. 1340) book *An Introduction and Elucidation of the Murder of the Martyr 'Uthman ibn 'Affan*. This work describes 'Uthman's virtues as found in *fada'il* works, but relies far more on selective historical narrative favorable to 'Uthman, rather than *hadith*, to create a cycle of martyrdom. The entire work is a vindication not only of 'Uthman, but of the first generation of Muslims. The divisions and trials that assailed the community were due to heretical fringe groups who either caused the revolt or later misrepresented the reasons for it. The book begins by defending 'Uthman and the Companions and concludes by condemning the *Rawafid*, who criticize the Companions and are therefore unbelievers. Any of the common criticisms held against 'Uthman as a reason for the siege, according to Ibn Bakr, are among the heresies of the *Rawafid*. His summary of these accusations and subsequent refutation of them are similar to those found in al-Muhibb al-Tabari and Ibn al-'Arabi. Like them he gives different interpretations or evidence whenever possible. And when not, he asserts, based on *hadith*, that if 'Uthman was a Companion and residing in Paradise then he simply could not have done the things for which he was accused. Ibn Bakr blames the revolt on the Saba'iyya who desired the *fitna* and caused the divisions within the community. Moreover, those who revolted against 'Uthman were judged by God and came to violent and untimely ends. In contrast, he repeatedly describes 'Uthman as being in Paradise with the Prophet and the first two caliphs and bearing the blood of martyrdom.

In his chapter on the siege and murder, Ibn Bakr contrasts 'Uthman's piety with the attackers' violence. Whereas earlier Ibn Bakr discredited the rebels as religious heretics, he now describes them as bandits motivated by a lust for revenge and greed. He augments the traditional accounts of al-Tabari, al-Baladhuri, and Ibn Sa'd so that his narrative of the murder goes on for ten pages. He dwells for some time on the image of 'Uthman weeping and praying as he read the Qur'an and being able to recite the Qur'an without making any mistakes despite the fierce battle that was raging around him. He also draws out the details of the battle in order to emphasize the amount of support for 'Uthman and the dedication of his defenders. He gives several accounts detailing how, when the rebels finally did break in, they were unable to kill 'Uthman after they saw him and talked with him. Once someone was finally able to strike the first blow, Ibn Bakr contrasts 'Uthman's piety and the attackers' brutality. They not only killed 'Uthman, but violated the religious privacy of his household, molested his women, and ransacked the public treasury.

The general point in presenting 'Uthman as a martyr is to defend the Companions and to insist 'Uthman was killed unjustly. But Ibn Bakr's extended treatment of 'Uthman's martyrdom suggests he was also crafting a martyr narrative to rival that of Husayn ibn 'Ali at Karbala, which was so constitutive for Shi'is, as well as the Christian martyrdom accounts that surrounded him in his home in Islamic Spain (al-Andalus). For example, Ibn Bakr claims 'Uthman's martyrdom was superior to 'Umar's and Husayn's was superior to 'Ali's because whereas 'Umar and 'Ali were killed in private by non-believers, the attack upon 'Uthman and Husayn lasted for a long time, was seen by everyone, and was carried out by those claiming to be fellow Believers. The idea of public witness certainly resonates with Christian martyr narratives. The emphasis on Believers who had been misled may reference Christian apostates betraying fellow Believers. Furthermore, 'Uthman's status as a martyr took on additional resonances in Islamic Spain as a part of legitimizing the Umayyad caliphate of Cordoba over and against the Fatimid caliphate in North Africa. In the congregational mosque in Cordoba a special ceremony was performed every Friday morning in which a large copy of the Qur'an, covered in engravings and kept in a special room, was brought out and taken in procession through the mosque, carried by two men because of its weight and preceded by a third man carrying a candle. It was claimed the Qur'an was one of the authoritative Qur'ans 'Uthman had ordered sent to the provinces, possibly Damascus. It also contained pages from 'Uthman's personal Qur'an that he had been reading when he was attacked and which had been splattered with his blood. In this ceremony 'Uthman's Qur'an became a relic commemorating a martyr to rival the reliquaries stored in the crypts of Spanish churches.

UNITY OF THE COMMUNITY

Through the exchange of letters and speeches chroniclers debated the question of who has the right, under what circumstances, to use force legitimately: rulers or rebels. 'Uthman's critics claimed they must resist and oppose 'Uthman out of obedience to God and the Qur'an. 'Uthman and his supporters argued for the unity of the community and that out of "fear of *fitna*" the ruler has the right, indeed the duty, to resist with force any who try to rise up against him. Whether such formulations had been worked out in 'Uthman's day seems highly unlikely. But once they were they were located within, and given additional symbolic force through, the controversy surrounding 'Uthman's caliphate. Many of the statements of 'Uthman's supporters reflect what became the dominant political philosophy of the 'Abbasid Court, what modern scholars refer to as Perso-Islamic kingship, a defense of Sasanian-style absolutism bolstered by Quranic appeals to God's sovereignty and the unity of the Community.

In addition to 'Uthman's specific abuses, critics declared 'Uthman an unjust ruler and an existential threat to a Quranic order. A letter from Qur'an readers (or village leaders) in Kufa stated that 'Uthman's governor had mistreated men of piety and virtue and concluded with the bold assertion: "You are our commander [*amir*] as long as you obey God and act uprightly." Another letter attributed to a dissident in Kufa stated:

> Authority [*imara*] over the believers only came to you by virtue of the *shura* when you made a pledge to God to follow the *sunna* of His Prophet and not to fall short of it. If they were to consult us about you a second time, we would transfer it [the *imara*] from you. O 'Uthman, the Book of God is for whomever it has reached and [whoever] has recited it; we have recited it just as you have. If the reciter [of the Quran] does not follow what is in it, it becomes an argument against him. (Al-Baladhuri, *Ansab al-ashraf*, 531)

Those in Egypt complaining about 'Uthman's policies, wrote to him urging him to remember God and His ordinances. They continued:

> So we remind you of God and we prohibit you from rebellion. For verily you called us to obedience and the Book of God and the Book of God notes: there is no obedience to one rebelling (against) God. Verily we were obedient to God by supporting and revering you, but then rejected that when we learned that you wanted to destroy us and destroy yourself. We must reject and disobey whoever keeps us from God. You are merely a mortal servant whereas God is the eternal creator. (Ibn Shabbah, *Tarikh al-medina al-munawwara*, 193)

These letters present authority as based upon the consent of the people and the leader's obedience to God's will as set out in the Qur'an.

While these may seem like compelling arguments, they actually serve to present 'Uthman's challengers as religious extremists—ultra puritans who come down in heresiographical literature as exemplars of religious extremism. From the Sunni viewpoint the opponents of 'Uthman foreshadow not only the partisans of 'Ali, but also the Kharijites, a future schismatic group who abandoned and condemned 'Ali after he agreed to the arbitration with Mu'awiya at Siffin. They argued that this was a terrible mistake and that as a result 'Ali had forfeited his right to be the leader. Although 'Ali defeated them in battle at Nahrawan (in 658) it was one of the survivors who later assassinated 'Ali. Kharijite became a byword for sedition and schism for Sunni and Shi'i Muslims alike. As the Kharijite idea developed it claimed leadership belonged to whoever was most worthy, and that worthiness was predicated on not falling into political or moral error. More problematically, they regarded Muslims who rejected their principles to be infidels. As a highly idealistic movement it inevitably fragmented and weakened as no leader could maintain support for long and disagreements emerged as to what constituted a significant error. But while ill equipped for exercising power or even overthrowing existing powers, the Kharijite concept has remained a thorn in the side of Islamic leaders.

In reaction to the dangerous ideas of condemning innovation as *bid'a* and the harvest of the first *fitna*, the Sunni majority adopted the principles of a group known as the Murji'ite, meaning to defer judgment (coming from Q 9:106). In some ways this was a reaffirmation of the central tenet of Islam—the oneness of God in which any claims to Godlike authority, wisdom, or association are condemned as idolatry. When applied to politics it meant it was not a Muslim's place to take sides on 'Uthman or the Civil War. Were the Companions right or wrong in their behavior? Were some more right than others? Only God knows and has the right to judge. There is still an obligation to judge right from wrong, a good Muslim from a bad one but, significantly, one cannot claim someone is not a Muslim at all based on his or her behavior. If someone self-identifies as a Muslim that is sufficient. While one can call Muslim individuals, groups, and leaders to reform or improve, one cannot regard them as "un-Islamic." This matters because Muslims are commanded to obey Muslim authorities whereas it is permissible, even commended, to wage *jihad* against un-Islamic ones. It meant an unjust ruler was still a Muslim "authority" deserving of obedience.

In contrast to 'Uthman's critics, who are tainted by association with schism and extremism, 'Uthman and his supporters defend his political authority based on Quranic passages and *hadith*. We can find both in letters and speeches by 'Uthman and his supporters. In Kufa when Sa'id ibn al-'As traveled to Medina with the other governors to confer with 'Uthman, his deputy confronted the crowds that were agitating against Sa'id and 'Uthman. He began by proclaiming the unity Islam had wrought among them was a blessing from God. Obedience to the ruler was necessary to maintain that unity. He stated: "O people, be still. For I heard the Messenger of God say, 'He who departs [from the Community] when there is a leader [*imam*] over the people'—and by God he did not say a just *imam*—'in order to shatter their staff and to break up their community, kill him whoever he may be'" (al-Tabari, *XV*, 140). Those who rebel against a leader are not seeking justice, but the break-up of the Community.

The Qur'an actually says very little about government but what it does say is utilized by 'Uthman and his supporters. During the siege and rebellion 'Uthman wrote several letters to dissidents in the garrison towns or to those gathered in Medina in which he cited Quranic verses that link obedience to the ruler with obedience to God. The verses remind the people they made a covenant with God when they promised to hear and obey, and those who break their oath will suffer a "painful chastisement." A letter also includes the ideologically key Quranic verse: "Obey God, and obey the Messenger and those in authority among you" (Q 4:59). 'Uthman warned them of the consequences of disobedience when he stated, "Verily you [pl.] will not find a community destroyed except from differences [among its members] and then it will not have a head unifying it. And when that happens you will not pray together and some of you will rule over the others and you will be divided into sects." A letter concludes with a verse urging them to avoid those who produce schisms and sects (Q 6:159). According to this argument, challenging the ruler leads to a divided community in which some factions rule over others. Obedience is the best way to avoid further oppression and division. Indeed, any who attack the ruler must be intent on destroying the unity of the community—regardless of what they may claim. Loyalty to the community and loyalty to the ruler (*imam*) are one and the same.

Central to 'Uthman's defense and reflective of understandings of kingship at the time, was God's sovereignty. The caliph refuses to abdicate on the grounds that he has been given the "cloak of authority" by God and it was not within his, or any ruler's, purview to remove it. The "cloak of authority" is a phrase that is repeated often in the confrontations between 'Uthman and his critics. God allowed the unjust ruler to reign and therefore it must be God's will and only He could remove him. This political philosophy was nearly universal in the pre-modern period; it helped to reconcile believing in God's sovereignty while living under tyranny. The ramifications of God's sovereignty in the Islamic context are similar to the "Mandate of Heaven" and "Divine Right Kingship" in medieval China and Europe respectively. Consider the Apostle Paul's exhortation to the Christians in Rome:

> Let everyone be subject to the governing authorities, for there is no authority except that which God has established. The authorities that exist have been established by God. Consequently, whoever rebels against the authority is rebelling against what God has instituted, and

those who do so will bring judgment on themselves. For rulers hold
no terror for those who do right, but for those who do wrong. Do you
want to be free from fear of the one in authority? Then do what is right
and you will be commended. For the one in authority is God's servant
for your good. But if you do wrong, be afraid, for rulers do not bear the
sword for no reason. They are God's servants, agents of wrath to bring
punishment on the wrongdoer. Therefore, it is necessary to submit to
the authorities, not only because of possible punishment but also as a
matter of conscience. (Romans 13:1–5)

This biblical passage insists upon obedience to the ruler, and Paul did
not specify a just ruler. Some Christians still cite these verses to justify
obeying political leaders, especially when their character or policies
would seem to argue against it.

The logic of the "cloak of authority" or "divine right kingship" was
to make those who rebelled against the existing authority also have to
rebel against God. However, if rebels were successful then the logic
flipped and their success became proof that God was on their side. But
this bait and switch was only possible after the fact. Thus, the outcome
of the attack upon the ruler was crucial. The outcome in 'Uthman's
case, and in most cases, was not greater justice, but anarchy and civil
war. Not surprisingly, our sources are keen to emphasize the consequence of attacking 'Uthman, and by extension any ruler, was *fitna*.
But chroniclers did not rush to this conclusion, they let 'Uthman's
besiegers have their say.

The besiegers insisted that 'Uthman's actions, not the success
of their protests, were proof that God had abandoned 'Uthman.
'Uthman continued to refer to his election in the *shura* council as the
foundation of his legitimacy, claiming it constituted a divine right to
rule since God had let him be chosen. The besiegers agreed in terms
of 'Uthman's election, and that based on his early conversion and status as a Companion of the Prophet he was worthy of authority, but
that since then he had changed and brought innovations. Furthermore,
when 'Uthman denied any knowledge of the letter and offered to make
any changes they desired the besiegers rejected this. They asserted
that if 'Uthman did write the letter than he was a liar and if he did
not then he was a weak leader, incapable of controlling his advisors

and administrators. In either case, he deserved to be deposed. He had become a test from God of whether the people would be faithful to the Qur'an and the example of Muhammad. In other words, 'Uthman's behavior and the sorry state of the Community must mean God had removed the mantle of authority from 'Uthman. The besiegers declared that the letter that 'Uthman supposedly wrote to his governor in Egypt breaking his covenant with them made 'Uthman's blood "lawful." He therefore had to either step down or they would kill him.

'Uthman insisted again that he could not step down because it was not within his power to remove the authority granted him by God. They would in fact have to fight and kill him. But he pointed out that according to the Qur'an it was only lawful to kill someone for one of three reasons: murder, apostasy, and adultery and he had done none of these things. God's sovereignty means a ruler cannot abdicate and injustice and corruption do not warrant the death penalty.

His besiegers, however, were not convinced and provided one last counter-argument. They replied:

> You mention the trials that will afflict us if we kill you. But it is not right to fail to uphold the truth against you out of fear of *fitna* sometime in the future. You say that it is lawful to kill a man only in three cases. But in the Book of God, we find that other men are put to death besides the three named by you. We find that the man who spreads corruption in the land [*hiraba*] is put to death, and likewise the oppressor who fights to continue his oppression and the man who prevents, resists, or battles against justice. (al-Tabari, *XV*, 222)

They listed 'Uthman's innovative and tyrannical policies one more time. They blamed him for bringing violence into the community by "clinging tenaciously" to power. If he would abdicate there would be no violence or division. He, 'Uthman, was the source of injustice and injustice was the source of *hiraba*. It was a mistake to acquiesce in the face of tyranny in the false hope of maintaining unity.

These exchanges culminate with the crucial question of when is it legitimate to use deadly force—either by the ruler against those threatening the unity of the community or by the people against an unjust ruler. At this point chroniclers turned to *hadith* about *fitna* to condemn rebellion. For example, 'Uthman paraphrased a *hadith* warning: "if you kill me, you will place the sword upon your necks, and Almighty God will not lift it from you until the Day of Resurrection. Do not kill me, for if you do, you will never pray together again, nor will you ever join together in sharing out booty nor will God ever remove dissension from among you." Not only will killing a ruler permanently divide the Community (as it did in 'Uthman's case), it will lead to more bloodshed. Another commonly cited *hadith* states that the unsheathed sword of God will kill 70,000 in a community that kills its prophet, while 35,000 will be killed if it kills a caliph. *Hadith* about the consequences of *fitna* became synonymous with 'Uthman's caliphate. They appear in *fada'il* works alongside those in which Muhammad praises 'Uthman's virtues. They also appear in chronicles as a final commentary on 'Uthman's caliphate and murder. Ibn Sa'd, the author of our earliest extant biography of 'Uthman, has a sub-section at the end of his biography entitled "mention of what the Companions of the Messenger of God said." In it 'Uthman's death is described as a permanent rupture or tear in Islam. It was also an event which had stripped the caliphate away from Muhammad's community so that leadership became no more than secular kingship. While the lens of faith can accept Muhammad's statements about 'Uthman's martyrdom or the *fitna* as prophetic, the lens of history suggests these kinds of *hadith* proliferated in the first few centuries of Islam as a way to legitimize particular religious or political opinions. It was the consequences of the revolt against 'Uthman that elicited these attitudes that were then attributed to Muhammad and located within the rebellion against 'Uthman to give them greater symbolic force.

Although religious scholars discouraged rebellion, they did not simply acquiesce in the face of tyranny. The main mechanism developed by Muslims for resisting or restraining the abuses of rulers was the law itself. Theoretically the ruler was subject to the divine law, *shari'a*, based on the Qur'an and the example of Muhammad, just like everyone else. We see this idea in action with 'Uthman in the interrogation before his election and when Companions and religious leaders criticized 'Uthman for diverting from the practice of his predecessors in everything from prayer to payroll. If "obey those in authority" is the most frequently cited verse from the Qur'an in relation to government, it has to be held in tension with what is perhaps the most frequently repeated theme in the Qur'an: the call to command what is right and forbid what is evil.

Through Quranic exegesis scholars sought ways to retain a check on authoritarian and arbitrary rule while still upholding the unity of the community. One of the ways they did this was by drawing a legal distinction between rebellion and banditry based on two Quranic verses. The rebellion, or *baghy*, verse is as follows:

> If two groups of believers come to fight one another, promote peace between them. Then if one of them turns aggressive [*baghat*] against the other, fight against the aggressive party till it returns to God's authority. If it does so, make peace among them equitably and be impartial. Verily God loves those who are just. The faithful are surely brothers; so restore friendship among your brothers and fear God that you may be favored. (Q 49:9–10)

Jurists interpreted this verse to mean if a group's disobedience was motivated by a religious interpretation (*tawil*), even if deemed heretical, this was different than brigandage motivated by greed and spreading chaos. They also argued that if one had a religious interpretation one was sincere, though perhaps misguided, in seeking change. The former group, as rebels, could be resisted, but still had protected rights. For example, they should not be held responsible for life or property destroyed in the course of the political agitation and fighting, and if they surrendered or retreated, their property should be restored to them and captives should not be killed or sold as slaves. This was a remarkably progressive attitude towards those who resisted or rose up against the established government. Additional attributes that characterized *baghy* were the need for a significant number to be involved in the protest. The rationale was that if there were many people there was probably a genuine grievance. Second, a large number meant that there was a greater chance of success in bringing about the desired change.

The *baghy* verse was contrasted with the *hiraba* verse, which is as follows:

> The punishment for those who wage war [*yuharibun*] against God and His prophet, and perpetrate disorders in the land, is to kill or hang them, or

have a hand on one side and a foot on the other cut off, or banish them
from the land. Such is their disgrace in the world, and in the hereafter
their doom shall be dreadful. But those who repent before they are
subdued should know that God is forgiving and kind. (Q 5:33–34)

So, what constitutes waging war against God and perpetrating disorder
in the land? Islamic jurists applied this verse to robbers and bandits,
those motivated by greed and those whose actions spread indiscrimi-
nate fear or terror. For example, highway robbery halts the wheels of
safe commerce—producing chaos. Attacking a member of a minority
makes all members of that minority terrified, which bears some similarities to modern western conceptions of terrorism and elicits similarly harsh punishments. Jurists, while not encouraging rebellion,
sought to shield those who criticized or rebelled against injustice from
being labeled *muharibun* and subject to death. Rebels still needed to be
stopped, they were a threat to the stability of the community. Jurists
were functioning within a "legal imperative" that by its nature favors
order and stability, but these were not the only political and moral
values taken into consideration. When the cost in blood and treasure
of pursuing greater justice seemed so high, restrained accommodation
might be the best option. But those who dared to confront the unjust
ruler were to be afforded legal protection; they were political prisoners not criminals. Motivation, methods, and outcomes determined
which was which.

The distinction between *baghy* and *hiraba* was informed by the
revolt against 'Uthman and then projected back into the confrontations between 'Uthman and his critics. The letter that 'Uthman
reportedly wrote to his governor in Egypt, ordering him to cut off the
hands and feet and hang those who had come to Medina to confront
'Uthman, labeled those men not rebels with legitimate grievances,
but criminals. This also helps explain why authors like Sayf ibn 'Umar
repeatedly asserted that those criticizing and then attacking 'Uthman
were seeking to profit from chaos and division. Nevertheless, as shown
above, al-Tabari included an account that attributes to the besiegers
the counter-argument that the unjust ruler, in this case 'Uthman, is
the one guilty of *hiraba*. But in the narratives of 'Uthman's caliphate it
is a lone voice, not often repeated, whereas the resounding refrain is

threats of *fitna*. Those who oppose the government are criminals or at best rebels, in which case they may have some protections, but they must be resisted—for the unity and stability of the community.

Ibn Khaldun the great fourteenth-century North-African historian and sociologist refers to this *hadith* in the volume-length introduction, *The Muqaddimah*, to his multi-volume history of the world. He analyzes the strength of dynasties and the feasibility of reformers changing or overthrowing them. He postulates that kingdoms pass through phases similar to those of an individual, from youthful vigor to dotage and senility. In the final stage brought about by the comfort and laziness that follows success, the kingdom is overthrown by a rival group that has not only more energy, but more of what he called *asabiyya*, tribal or group solidarity. Kingdoms are firmly entrenched and so it is extremely difficult to overthrow them. Reformers that try generally do not have adequate support, their piety having led them to withdraw from society. Lacking the wider support needed, the reformer perishes in the attempt. Reforms are a "divine matter that materializes only with God's pleasure and support, through sincere devotion for Him and in view of good intentions toward the Muslims" (Ibn Khaldun, *Muqaddimah*, 127). In this context he references the *hadith* frequently used to qualify the Quranic injunction to command the good and forbid evil. "Should one of you see evil activities, he should change them with his hand. If he cannot do that, he should change them with his tongue. And if he cannot do that, he should change them with his heart." If forbidding with the mouth or the hand would produce no good because it had little chance of success, while causing other evils, such as one's own death (suicide is forbidden in Islam), murder, or social chaos, then it is enough to forbid in one's heart. Here we see again that religion offers little ideological support for would-be rebels—until after their rebellion has succeeded and become a revolution. According to Ibn Khaldun those who have attempted reform, not realizing their need for "group solidarity" for success, are deluded and their enterprise is doomed to fail. Therefore, they should be either mocked for the insane fools that they are or punished "by execution or beatings when they cause trouble" (Ibn Khaldun, *Muqaddimah*, 128). It is important to note that Ibn Khaldun's prescriptive statement of what should happen emerges from his descriptive observations on what does happen.

CONCLUSION

In most of the early accounts of the rebellion against 'Uthman he comes across as arrogant or indecisive. He does not understand the animosity that his policies have generated. Too late he offered to repent and make changes and even then, there is the suggestion that this was disingenuous as 'Uthman struggled and schemed to hold on to power. However, *hadith* assert 'Uthman was a righteous Companion, affirmed by Muhammad and fated to die a martyr. To prove this a counter-narrative developed that presents 'Uthman as having pious intentions and just policies throughout his caliphate. The Companions did not abandon 'Uthman or turn on him, rather they were caught off guard by the vehemence and violence of a marginal few. In the counter-narrative of 'Uthman as a martyr, the image of the *Sahaba* as Muhammad's revered Companions is strengthened rather than threatened. So too was the link between criticizing the Companions and (Shi'i) heresy.

The ways in which 'Uthman's actions likely divided the early community were matched by greater emphasis on the unity of the (Sunni) Muslim Community. Those sources that use 'Uthman as a symbolic caliph more than a symbolic Companion get to a similar end, the importance of the unity of the Community (*umma*), by a different route. The lessons are clear: for rulers, criticism culminates in conflict, and for the ruled, better to tolerate tyranny than risk anarchy. Indeed, a phrase that became synonymous with medieval Arabic political philosophy was: "sixty years of tyranny is better than one day of anarchy." But this is a statement condemning anarchy not defending tyranny. It should be held in tension with the prophetic *hadith*: "one day of just rule by an equitable Sultan is more meritorious than sixty years of continual worship." We can see the apparent choice between tyranny and anarchy as the shadow side of a desire for unity and justice. These two aspirations are enshrined in the Qur'an and the life of Muhammad and yet came into conflict during the reign of 'Uthman ibn 'Affan.

In the second narrative strategy addressing the revolt against 'Uthman, there is an awareness of an inherent tension and consequently debates about how to resolve it. In modern parlance some historians were daring to ask: was 'Uthman a martyr killed by terrorists, or was he a tyrant who had to be forcefully removed for the sake of justice? Or, to put it another way: "is one person's terrorist, another person's freedom fighter?" Is there room for the freedom fighter, the revolutionary, in Islamic discourse, or is everyone who challenges or confronts a ruler a terrorist who will unleash chaos? Medieval scholars could not conceive of a freedom fighter or a revolutionary, but they did seek to distinguish political dissidents from common criminals. And although rejected by rulers and scholars alike, historians made the case articulated by 'Uthman's besiegers that it was possible for the tyrannical ruler to threaten rather than safeguard communal unity, to be the source of evil rather than the enforcer of good. In other words, they raised at least the possibility of what today would be called "state terrorism." Importantly, they concluded that this was not the case with 'Uthman because he was a Companion, but also because the consequences of the rebellion against 'Uthman—bloodshed, civil war, schism, and chaos—were so disastrous. But what if the consequences had been different?

7

CONTESTED CONTINUITY

INTRODUCTION

In the last chapter we saw how writers from the eighth to the fourteenth centuries were writing history that they could use in the present. All communities and nations create a "usable past" that evolves in response to changing circumstances. The past can be interpreted in a way that defends traditional boundaries and values that appear threatened by changing circumstances. It can also be interpreted in ways that provide a historical pedigree and cultural authenticity to what are otherwise new communal identities and values. In the Islamic context the history of 'Uthman ibn 'Affan has been used to defend well-established communal and ideological boundaries down to the present. It has also been used to support modern reform movements.

The significance of many of the chapters in 'Uthman's life continues to reverberate in the modern Islamic world. These include the contradictory assessment of the Companions by Sunnis and Shi'is, the authenticity of 'Uthman's Quranic codex, 'Uthman's succession to the caliphate through a selection process, and the rebellion that ended his caliphate and his life. By way of conclusion this chapter looks at how the medieval consensus in each of these areas has been contested or reimagined in the last century and yet in each case proven incredibly resilient. It is impossible within a single chapter to look at the modern Islamic world as a whole. While the *umma* as the unified Community of Believers continues to resonate, it has been checked by the rise of the nation state and distinct regional developments: another example of contested continuity. Accordingly, this chapter focuses for the most part on events, authors, and activists in Egypt as a way of illustrating how modern debates and developments interface with the legacy of 'Uthman. In other words, we are looking once again at a world that is "made by" 'Uthman and continually "remaking" 'Uthman.

COMPANION

This book has argued consistently that defending the Companions, including 'Uthman and those who elected him, became constitutive of Sunni identity. All the Companions needed to be perceived as righteous, unified, and above reproach in order to prevent further fracturing of the Sunni community, to legitimize *hadith* and *hadith* scholars, and to refute Shi'i claims. Early Islamic history was crafted and then interpreted to support these aims. But in the modern period, with first the Great Powers of Europe and then the Cold War Superpowers pursuing policies of "divide and rule," in the Muslim world there were calls for Sunni–Shi'i rapprochement and mutual cooperation. In the mid-twentieth century Al-Azhar University in Cairo established a committee, led by Mahmud Shaltut, to explore Sunni–Shi'i dialogue and reconciliation. This group argued that Sunnis and Shi'is should work together because what divided them, namely differing views of the Companions and the caliphate, was less significant than what united them: shared commitment to the Qur'an as God's Message and Muhammad as God's Messenger.

The members of the ecumenical committee discussed whether it was necessary to tackle the divergent views of early Islamic history held by Sunnis and Shi'is. Mahmud Fayyad called for a revision of the study and writing of history that would be free from the "fanaticism and falsehood" that had characterized earlier historiography. He insisted they needed to study the past objectively, determine what happened, and move forward. He recognized that the narratives of early Islamic history were influenced by the evolution of sectarian identities in the eighth and ninth centuries and he wanted a history that could foster Sunni–Shi'i reconciliation and collaboration. But how to write a more useful and supposedly "objective" history? On what basis and using which sources? Other scholars argued that tackling the differing opinions of early Islamic history in general, and the behavior of the Companions in particular, would cause more problems than it would solve. They pointed out it was impossible to change the past and difficult to change the (hi)stories written about the past, and therefore it was best to just ignore the past and focus on the present. This was the view that won out on the committee.

Sunnis and Shi'is actually agree on many of the details of 'Uthman's life and yet come to very different conclusions about their significance. As seen in previous chapters the historical material accepted by Sunnis provides plenty of material with which to condemn 'Uthman, from his cowardice at the Battle of Badr to his corrupt government appointees, from the machinations surrounding his election to the caliphate, to the duplicitous dealings with his critics at the end of his caliphate. Sunnis also assert 'Uthman was a beloved Companion of the Prophet, elected by the consensus of the *shura* members and endorsed by the Community; his caliphate was overthrown by a conspiracy movement led by the heretic, 'Abdallah ibn Saba'. Shi'is do not see things the same way. In terms of 'Uthman's character, they regard 'Uthman's acts of generosity as not particularly noteworthy. They believe Muhammad chose 'Uthman to represent him to the Quraysh in the lead up to the Treaty of Hudaybiyya because 'Uthman was accepted by Muhammad's fiercest Umayyad opponent, Abu Sufyan, hardly something about which to boast. Significantly, Shi'is reject the appellation "*Dhu al-nurayn*" ("Possessor of the two lights"), arguing the two women 'Uthman married were not Muhammad's biological daughters, but his wives' daughters from their previous marriages. These two daughters were married to non-believers before they were married to 'Uthman; Shi'is argue Muhammad would not have done this with his own daughters. They also point out that there is no evidence of Muhammad having a close relationship with these "daughters" or of them aiding Muhammad in any way, unlike his daughter, Fatima, who was married to 'Ali.

In terms of 'Uthman's caliphate, as seen in Chapter 3, the election of 'Uthman rather than 'Ali to be the third caliph is a particularly contentious issue between the two communities. Sunni tradition came to downplay or ignore the accounts that portray the *shura* participants negatively, in favor of accounts that present a smooth and unanimous transition of power to 'Uthman. In contrast, Shi'is focus on the machinations and the intimations that they were designed to prevent 'Ali from becoming caliph. Shi'is insist 'Ali only accepted the election of 'Uthman because he knew to resist it would lead to conflict, and very likely a bloody one. Shi'is do not refer to accounts that blame 'Abdallah ibn Saba'; instead they point to those in which 'Ali interceded on 'Uthman's behalf with the delegation of protestors who traveled from Egypt to Medina to confront 'Uthman, and that 'Ali insisted 'Uthman's household received water once the siege had begun. 'Ali only abandoned 'Uthman to his fate after 'Uthman repeatedly failed to honor the promises he had made to the people. For Shi'is, 'Ali defended 'Uthman because he accepted the first three caliphs as rulers and administrators without renouncing his own claim to be Muhammad's heir and inheritor (*wasi*), his legitimate successor in its full and proper meaning. Like 'Ali, Shi'is can criticize the Companions for not following the true path and endorsing 'Ali as Muhammad's only true successor, but that does not mean they have to curse the compromised Companions or deny the good things that happened during their reigns, such as the rapid expansion of Islam.

Shi'is believe all people, including the Companions, should be evaluated based on their actions and they then divide the Companions into three categories. The first group were those who never disagreed with Muhammad or faltered in their commitment to Islam. The second group were Companions who lapsed in their devotion or obedience, and the third group were apostates or false Companions. Shi'is interpret phrases like: "those among them who believe and do righteous deeds" in Qur'an 48:29 as referring to the Companions, meaning that some of Muhammad's Companions did not believe or do righteous deeds. Or consider Qur'an 9:38–39, "O you who have believed, what is [the matter] with you that, when you are told to go forth in the cause of Allah, you cling heavily to the earth? Are you satisfied with the life of this world rather than the Hereafter? ... If you do not go forth, He will punish you with a painful punishment and will replace you with another people." Significantly, Shi'is interpret this to mean that the Companions could be condemned, both by God and the true Believers; one moment of belief or act of faithfulness does not count for eternity. In contrast, Sunnis interpret passages like these as praising those Jews and Christians who are accepted by God, condemning those few Companions who followed Muhammad but lacked genuine belief, or referring to momentary mistakes by Companions that were later forgiven. Sunni *hadith* referring to the "Ten Promised Paradise" and the Sunni corpus of "virtues" and "merit" literature secures the individual and collective reputation of the Companions, including 'Uthman.

Al-Azhar's ecumenical committee chose to focus on cooperation in the present without addressing the disagreements over the past; its efforts were given official support by the Egyptian president Gamal Abdel Nasser, leader of the non-aligned movement and *bête noire* of the British. Nasser saw that Iran and Egypt faced a common threat in Britain as Iran nationalized its oil industry and Egypt nationalized the Suez Canal. With Nasser's support, Mahmud Shaltut became Shaykh of al-Azhar in 1958 and in 1959 Shaltut issued a religious legal ruling (*fatwa*) recognizing both the Zaydi and Imami schools of Shi'i jurisprudence (*madhhab*) to be as legitimate as the four Sunni legal schools, and a part of the curriculum at al-Azhar. This act proclaimed the Shi'is to be members of a different sect, but fellow Muslims. While this continues to be the official stance of al-Azhar, it has had very limited impact on Sunni–Shi'i relations. Other members of al-Azhar strongly opposed the work of the ecumenical committee and argued Shi'ism was more than a different sect, but a different religion and a religion that posed an existential threat to true (Sunni) Islam.

In 1960, after Shaltut's *fatwa* and in an effort to thwart the ecumenical movement, Muhibb al-din al-Khatib (d. 1969) wrote a pamphlet condemning Shi'ism as a separate and false religion. Muhibb al-Din was an influential Salafi journalist and publisher. He fused religion, politics, and ethno-nationalism in his arguments. It was 'Abdallah ibn Saba' who plotted against the early Community, attempted to pit the Companions against each other, and conspired in the murder of 'Uthman ibn 'Affan that caused the Community to descend into civil war. He echoed medieval Sunni heresiographies that the teachings by 'Abdallah ibn Saba' about 'Ali were the beginning of Shi'ism. Furthermore, he doubled down on the centrality of the vaulted view of the Companions. If it was possible for the Companions to go astray, to put their own worldly ambitions, for example in the case of 'Uthman's election, before the good of the Community, then Muhammad's mission would appear to have failed within a generation. For Salafis the virtuous character of Abu Bakr, 'Umar, 'Uthman, and 'Ali and the unity of the early Community are essential proofs of the truth of Islam. This view has been extremely influential in shaping the views of Sunni Muslims today.

Before the ecumenical movement, Salafism emerged in the late nineteenth and early twentieth centuries arguing that the first Muslims, the pious ancestors, or al-salaf al-salih, were the truest embodiment of Islam and needed to be emulated. Salafism is a tricky term because different groups and generations of Salafis highlight different attributes for emulation. By the late-twentieth century Salafism was primarily a conservative movement calling for strict adherence to shari'a law and emulation of the Prophet's actions in all areas. However, originally, in the early twentieth century, the Salafiya movement sought to modernize Islam. According to these Salafis, the Muslim world had fallen to European powers because Muslims had focused on actions rather than attitudes. Like the "Righteous Ancestors," modern Muslims needed to be willing to evaluate political, social, and religious traditions and customs, and if they were proven false or found wanting, replace them with the truth. True Islam would not contradict science or social welfare. European Imperialists and Orientalists criticized Islam and Islamic societies for being despotic, stagnant, and superstitious and then used that characterization to justify Europe's "civilizing mission." Early Salafis accepted the criticism but sought to combat European imperialism by arguing authentic Islamic civilization was, in fact, the opposite. In order to be successful in the modern world, Muslims did not need to emulate Europeans, but Muhammad and the Companions—as the Salafis presented them. Influenced by early Salafism, for example, a group of Muslim reformers in the 1930s and 1940s argued the prophetic period exemplified the modern liberal values of personal freedom, reason, and democracy. They sought to convince their conservative compatriots of this by writing historical biographies in which being politically democratic was added to the list of timeless character traits and pious virtues of Muhammad and the Companions. This modern form of "virtues" and "merits" literature became known as *Islamiyyat*. In it 'Uthman ibn 'Affan became both a proof and a test of early Islamic democracy.

CONSULTATION

Two prominent intellectuals who wrote *Islamiyyat* works on 'Uthman ibn 'Affan are Taha Husayn and 'Abbas Mahmud al-'Aqqad. Taha Husayn (d. 1973) was one of the greatest twentieth-century Egyptian intellectuals. Despite being from a poor village in upper Egypt and blind from the age of three, he attained a PhD from the Sorbonne and became a professor of literature and history at Cairo University, and later the Minister of Education. Among his sixty publications, he wrote a two-volume work entitled *The Great Fitna*; the first volume on 'Uthman ibn 'Affan was published in 1947 and the second, on 'Ali ibn 'Abi Talib and his sons, was published in 1952. Anxious about the corruption of the ruling elite and the suffering of the poor, Taha Husayn used the history of the *fitna* to argue that the resources for social change can be found within Islam. 'Abbas Mahmud al-'Aqqad (d. 1964) was born the same year as Taha Husayn and was also from upper Egypt, the city of Aswan. Unlike Taha Husayn, he had little in the way of formal education, not progressing past elementary school; nevertheless, he was a polymath. He was a prominent intellectual, literary critic, newspaper columnist, and prolific writer. He wrote over a hundred books, fifty of those were on history, the most prominent being a series of historical biographies under the title "Geniuses of Islam," including one on 'Uthman ibn 'Affan. Outside both the western and Islamic education system, al-'Aqqad saw himself as the self-appointed defender of Islamic civilization from the attacks of orientalists and extremists. He wanted to instill in people a sense of pride in their Islamic heritage that would empower them to improve themselves and their country. Al-'Aqqad did become the intellectual of the people. His biographies shaped many people's first impression of Islamic history and from the late 1950s they were a standard part of many Arabic language curricula.

Taha Husayn and al-'Aqqad, in addition to arguing that early Islam was democratic in principle, present 'Uthman's election by a consultative council as an example of the democratic process in action. Both Husayn and al-'Aqqad praise 'Umar for establishing the consultative council. Al-'Aqqad sees the *shura* as evidence of 'Umar's "constitutionalism." According to al-'Aqqad, if anyone could have appointed the right man to succeed himself and convince the people of this, it was 'Umar, and yet he chose the method of *shura*; this proves that election is better than appointment. In fact, he makes the point that 'Umar became outraged at the suggestion he should appoint his son to succeed him. Furthermore, it did not matter that it was not a general election because 'Umar knew the six men of the *shura* council were the only ones who aspired to the caliphate. Taha Husayn describes 'Umar's rule as offering the perfect balance between socialism and capitalism, but that his efforts to establish this ideal social system failed because he was ahead of his time. Nevertheless, Taha Husayn is compelled to ask why 'Umar did not widen the *shura* to include everyone and so establish a true "parliamentary system"? Taha Husayn believes that the evidence of 'Umar's life suggests that he would and could have completed this key political transition had it not been for his untimely death. However, after his fatal stabbing 'Umar was forced to speed up the process from his deathbed and at that point a consultative council was what was possible. For Taha Husayn this missed opportunity is a tragedy of mammoth proportions. That 'Umar was prevented from putting into place the "guarantee or protection" needed to "maintain the relationship" of mutual accountability that is at the heart of democracy became apparent during 'Uthman's reign.

Both authors turn the account of the *shura* into a civics primer on how to run a parliamentary election, and a commentary on the state of Egypt's own fledgling democracy. Al-'Aqqad notes that some might criticize the *shura* for introducing competition and divisions, as well as raising false expectations for five of them of acquiring the caliphate.

However, al-'Aqqad insists it is only natural to compete for even the least post and there is nothing wrong with this rivalry or competition. Moreover, it quickly became clear who was the best person, with the field narrowing to 'Ali and 'Uthman and majority opinion finally settling on 'Uthman. Taha Husayn emphasizes that the six *shura* members did ask the people for their preference—and not just men; they also asked the opinion of honorable women and in particular the wives of the Prophet, the "*Ummahat al-Mu'minin*." Both authors present the *shura* in a way that looks remarkably similar to modern European parliamentary elections, in which multiple candidates compete in the first round of elections and there is then a run-off election between the top two candidates.

Al-'Aqqad rejects any account that would cast aspersions on either the method or members of the *shura*. He admits there are accounts that tell of various machinations by the *shura* members, but he insists these are biased and without merit, or "fabrications designed to deceive the deceivable." Al-'Aqqad also suggests that they may have been contrived and recorded to create a more theatrical story or made up by Orientalists. In contrast, Taha Husayn relates the divisions and disagreements among the *shura* members and 'Ali's reluctance to give the oath of allegiance to 'Uthman. But they both argue that Islam properly understood and practiced is not only compatible with modern democratic values, but embodied those values long before the Europeans.

So why according to these authors did this early democratic experiment fail? Taha Husayn blames the elite. He states: "Islam made everyone equal in rights and obligations, but the conquests brought new privileges and within hours of Muhammad's death there was a new aristocracy" of the tribe of Quraysh. According to Taha Husayn, Abu Bakr and 'Umar never intended to prioritize the Quraysh, but rather the first converts to Islam. Society continued to stray from the "Muhammadan ideal" with the strains and changes brought about by the conquests. For example, Taha Husayn echoes ninth-century chronicles as he describes the problems in the province city of Kufa as an alliance between old and new elites. But he translates the tribalism of late antiquity into the class conflict of the twentieth century. He blames corruption in 'Uthman's government for growing discrepancies between an "idle, luxurious aristocratic class and a class of slaves doing all the work." The democratic experiment failed because the necessary safeguards had not been put in place; there was no legitimate mechanism for the people to express their grievances or check the abuses of the ruling elite.

In contrast, Al-'Aqqad attributes the rebellion against 'Uthman to the arrogance of the people stemming from the new rights they had won from Islam and which 'Uthman bestowed on them. The "kindness of 'Uthman emboldened them and seduced them" and made them susceptible to the schemes of "doubters and grumblers." He stops his narrative short of the final stages of the revolt and siege, summarizing them as "ugly" and insignificant. He states that he does not want to dwell on these details, claiming it is enough to say that all the historians point to a conspiracy led by 'Abdallah ibn Saba', a Jewish convert turned heretic. Similarly, Muhammad Husayn Haykal (d. 1956), whose biography of Muhammad launched the *Islamiyyat* effort, started a biography of 'Uthman around 1945 but never wrote the final chapter on the siege and revolt. Ahmed Amin (d. 1954), a prominent historian, social commentator, and prolific writer, wrote a three-volume history of Islamic civilization in which he briefly summarizes the revolt against 'Uthman as a conspiracy led by 'Abdallah ibn Saba'. Thus, while the virtues attributed to the Companions were essentially modern, the method of idealizing the Companions was closer to medieval "merits" and "virtues" literature than modern historical source criticism. As western scholars took up the challenge of the historical record for early Islam, another core aspect of 'Uthman's legacy came under scrutiny: the authenticity of 'Uthman's Quranic codex.

CALIPHATE

Muslims' belief in an "early" Qur'an that was authoritative during Muhammad's lifetime and codified during 'Uthman's reign came under attack in the 1970s by western scholars arguing for either a "Late Qur'an" or a "pre-Qur'an." The "late Qur'an" thesis is that the Qur'an did not take final form until the late-eighth or early-ninth century, in other words 100 to 200 years after Muhammad. John Wansbrough, a chief proponent of this view, posited that a large body of oral traditions circulated and proliferated after Muhammad's death until at that relatively late date some were determined to be authoritative and canonical and gathered into the Qur'an while others were jettisoned. In other words, the Qur'an followed a similar pattern of development as the *hadith* literature. Furthermore, this process was in response to the "sectarian milieu" of Abbasid Baghdad in which Jews, Christians, Zoroastrians, Believers, and non-Believers dialogued and debated with each other. Only as the doctrines and practices of a distinct Muslim identity and community were defined and defended in this competitive arena were the Qur'an and *hadith* codified and canonized. The "late Qur'an" thesis shook the scholarly community and elicited stinging condemnation in the Muslim world where it was seen as an imperialistic power play against Islam.

In recent decades the evidence for the 'Uthmanic Qur'an described in the Islamic historical tradition has grown. In 1972 a collection of ancient manuscripts of the Qur'an, some dating from the late-seventh century, was discovered in the Great Mosque in Sana, Yemen. They have been the subject of painstaking preservation and study ever since. Likewise, study of the Quranic inscriptions on the Dome of the Rock in Jerusalem built on the orders of the Umayyad caliph 'Abd al-Malak at the end of the seventh century indicate a community familiar with a set Quranic corpus. Finally, unlike *hadith*, the Qur'an has no anachronistic references, which is hard to imagine if the Qur'an was produced 200 years after the events of early Islamic history, especially the first *fitna* and split between Sunni and Shi'i. The differences between the Qur'an and *hadith* point to different historical contexts not a similar one. The other argument put forward for a late Qur'an was that the Qur'an assumes its audience is familiar with biblical characters and themes. However, a current vibrant area of study is the cross-pollination between Near Eastern religions in late antiquity, including the Arabian Peninsula of the seventh century. Indeed, it is what is giving force to the argument for a "pre-Qur'an."

The "pre-Qur'an" idea also hit the field of Quranic studies like a bombshell in the 1970s through the work of Gunter Luling. Those following in Luling's footsteps pay close attention to the phrasing and philology of the Qur'an, finding more and more evidence of Syriac loan words, phrases, and technical terms associated with Nestorian Christians using a Syro-Aramaic liturgical language. In the hands of some, this has led to a reductionist view of the Qur'an that is presented as little more than a corruption of Judeo-Christian Syriac hymnody and liturgical texts—thus the idea of a "pre-Qur'an." However, a growing body of micro studies on particular passages, phrasing, vocabulary, and themes in the Qur'an point to engagement with and creative redeployment of Christian themes and "syriacisms" to produce a distinctly Quranic, that is Islamic, understanding of God and His relationship with humanity. The Qur'an is increasingly studied by those with linguistic and cultural knowledge of late antiquity, not just medieval Arabic and Islam. But as scholars distance their analysis from the Islamic Quranic commentaries that date, like *hadith* and historical narratives, from the ninth century, new aspects of life in seventh-century Arabia are emerging. For example, one in which Muhammad was interacting with and appealing to monotheists in Arabia, including Mecca, as much or more as he was to polytheists. Even as studies uphold the Islamic version of events surrounding the 'Uthmanic codex they highlight how tenuous is our ability to recreate the world of the first generation of Muslims as the controversies surrounding 'Uthman so powerfully illustrate.

CRISIS

Perhaps the other most enduring legacy of 'Uthman's caliphate is the "fear of *fitna*" arguments developed by medieval scholars in response to the rebellion against 'Uthman. As we have seen, the danger of *fitna* was used to condemn the rebellion against 'Uthman in particular, and eventually against the ruler in general. Although temporarily tested during the mass uprisings of the 2011 "Arab Spring," the logic and efficacy of "fear of *fitna*" found new resonance during the turbulent aftermath.

During the eighteen days of protests against the regime of Egyptian President Mubarak, key leaders at al-Azhar denounced the demonstrators on the basis of *fitna*. Ahmad al-Tayyib, shaykh of al-Azhar since 2010, and 'Ali Gomaa, grand mufti of Egypt from 2003 to 2013, told Egyptians that the Qur'an is clear: obey those in authority over you; to rebel against the legitimate ruler is a sin that will lead to *fitna*. Gomaa quoted *hadith* warning that God damns those who stir up *fitna*. Gomaa and Al-Tayyib chastised the youth for not being grateful when Mubarak offered to dialogue with them. They urged protesters to believe Mubarak when he promised to make changes, to go home, and to let the legitimate ruler do his job. It was hard, however, to make the accusations of *fitna* stick, in part because the protestors did not resort to violence or threaten national unity, in fact they did the opposite. Demonstrators adopted the symbol of a crescent and a cross—Islam and Christianity—that had been a part of the Egyptian nationalist movement against British imperialism at the beginning of the twentieth century. They remained committed to non-violence in the face of government snipers and water cannons.

The government's tactics backfired, making it appear to be the source of division and violence in the country all along; and the tide turned against it. On February 11, 2011, after thirty years as president, Hosni Mubarak stepped down, or rather was pushed out, as military leaders informed him they would not shoot the demonstrators or defend him—it was time he left. The Supreme Command of the Armed Forces (SCAF) took over as an interim government until parliamentary and presidential elections could be held and a new constitution drafted.

Leaders at al-Azhar were compelled to defend their previous support for the Old Regime. Five days after Mubarak stepped down, Ahmad al-Tayyib, the shaykh of al-Azhar, made a public announcement clarifying al-Azhar's stance during the revolution. He argued al-Azhar had two main concerns: it did not want any blood to be spilt and it did not want division and schisms within the country. In this way he echoed the "fear of *fitna*" formula that had developed in response to the divisions that rocked the early Islamic community, and then been given rhetorical force in the recorded confrontations between 'Uthman and his besiegers.

The following fall, on October 11, 2011, al-Azhar issued a "Declaration in Support of the Arab Revolutions" that continues to warn against *fitna* even as it reframes the potential sources of *fitna*. It upholds the Quranic call for justice and unity when it states:

> The practice of many rulers, with aspirations to absolute power, is to cling to the incorrect understanding of the Quranic verse: "O you who have believed, obey Allah and obey the Messenger [Prophet Muhammad] and those of you who are in authority" (Surah Al-Nisâ: 4/59), ignoring its clear and obvious contextual meaning in the preceding verse which states: "verily Allah commands you to render back the trusts to whom they are due; and when you judge between people, to judge with justice" (Surah Al-Nisâ: 4/58). ... *those among our scholars who justified patience with tyrannical rulers, to ensure the well-being of the nation from chaos, have also allowed the ousting of the tyrannical oppressor if the people have the ability to achieve this and if there is no possibility of damage and harm to the nation and its communities.* [Emphasis mine] (www.dur.ac.uk/ilm/ newsarchive/?itemno=13661)

The non-violence, social solidarity, and success of the protests-turned-revolution meant it was not *fitna* and should not be condemned as the rebellion against 'Uthman had been. The Declaration continues by echoing the claims of 'Uthman's besiegers that it was the violent and reckless behavior of the government as it sought to preserve its hold on power that was the real threat to the country. It condemns the government for using stability and fear of *fitna* as a pretext for power. The regime lost its legitimacy when it used deadly force against the demonstrators because according to *shari'a* law this is only permissible against those who have committed murder or spread "corruption on earth" (*hiraba*).

But the declaration issues a warning to the revolutionaries as well. They could be demoted back to rebels guilty of *baghy* if their actions led to bloodshed or betrayed the nation through affiliation or influence from outside powers. The unity of the community remained paramount and a justification for counter-revolution. The document continues to express the desire for justice so long as it does not threaten national unity:

> The forces of the revolution and reform should unite in achieving their dream of justice and freedom. They should also avoid sectarian, ethnic, doctrinal and religious conflicts in order to preserve their national

fabric and respect citizens' rights... building a future based on equality and justice... They must prevent the uprising from being exploited by sectarianism or denominationalism.

These remarks sounded a warning as multiple countries in the region descended into civil war. In Egypt, attacks against Christians that had begun while the SCAF was in charge increased after the Muslim Brotherhood candidate, Muhammad Morsi, was elected president in 2012. The political uncertainty and economic hardship that accompany revolution, exacerbated by the president and parliament chosen for their ideology rather than their competency, helped to further pave the way for a counter-revolution. The growing sense of internal threat compounded by the wider violence in the region enabled the military, backed by the old guard, to rekindle the fear of *fitna*; and assert its authority once more. General Abdel Fattah al-Sisi, flanked by the shaykh of al-Azhar and the Coptic patriarch, announced on public television July 3, 2013, that he was removing Morsi from office. Al-Sisi was eventually elected president himself. His government has been more oppressive and intolerant than Mubarak's. Al-Sisi and the military, supported by the establishment, effectively deployed fear of *fitna* rhetoric and convinced many to accept tyranny as necessary to achieve stability and security.

CONCLUSION

In some sense the last two chapters have fallen victim to the same temptation that beset medieval Arab historians, allowing the symbolism of the rebellion against 'Uthman to overshadow, obscure, even erase 'Uthman as a person. To some extent, those historians make trying to do otherwise extremely difficult. But perhaps there was something about 'Uthman himself that made him disappear from the narrative of his own life. If there is any truth in the historical narratives, he was not a strong presence during Muhammad's lifetime. He did not have the will or ability to protect Muslims from Qurayshi persecution in Mecca. And this despite being a wealthy, and therefore presumably influential, member of the powerful Umayyad clan within

Quraysh. He was not known for his bravery in battle, in fact the oppo-site. He did not play a role in resolving the leadership crisis that faced the Community when Muhammad died. He hardly played a role in his own election to be the Commander of the Believers. More crucially, he failed to grasp the significance of his new position, continuing to act like a generous grandfather bestowing benefits on his family and favor-ites. To the extent that he did engage with directing resources towards the campaigns of conquest, at least by the second half of his rule, he appears exhausted by the effort. He failed to keep abreast of what was happening in the empire until it was too late. He was unable to rein in or reconcile the ambitions of the younger more dynamic men around him. In the end, if he was not duplicitous and tyrannical, he was at least indecisive and weak.

But 'Uthman also elicits a certain degree of sympathy and the sense that he did not deserve his death. He was a well-established man of commerce who had some form of conversion experience upon encountering Muhammad and his message. He rejected the beliefs of his community. Forced to flee to Ethiopia and then Medina, he risked losing everything. He was generous to his family and friends and per-haps in superlative ways to the early Community of Believers. He was gentle and did not like conflict, which was admired in his interpersonal relationships. After all, this was one of the reasons Muhammad married two of his daughters (or possibly stepdaughters) to 'Uthman. Although old and potentially frail by the end of his life, he helped to preserve and pursue a new Islamic regional order. And 'Uthman's legacy continues. His Quranic codex has held the Muslim Community together and provides one of our few Islamic sources from the first century of Islam. The lands he held and that were conquered during his reign continue to be those most closely associated with Islam.

'Uthman is a Maker of the Muslim World both for his accomplish-ments and for how the Community has responded to his failures.

SELECTED BIBLIOGRAPHY

MODERN SCHOLARSHIP

Abou El Fadl, Khaled. *Rebellion & Violence in Islamic Law*. Cambridge, UK: Cambridge University Press, 2001; reprint, 2002.

Afsaruddin, Asma. "In Praise of the Caliphs: Re-Creating History from the Manaqib Literature." *International Journal of Middle East Studies* 31:3 (1999): 329–350.

_____. *Striving in the Path of God: Jihad and Martyrdom in Islamic Thought*. Oxford: Oxford University Press, 2013.

Al-'Aqqad, 'Abbas Muhammad. *Al-'Abqariyyat al-islamiyya*. Beirut: Dar al-kitab al-lubnani, 1994.

Bell, Richard and W. Montgomery Watt. *Bell's Introduction to the Qur'ān*. Edinburgh: Edinburgh University Press, 1994.

Brunner, Rainer. *Islamic Ecumenism in the 20th Century: Azhar and Shiism Between Rapprochement and Restraint*. Leiden: Brill, 2004.

Busool, Assad N. "The Development of Taha Husayn's Islamic Thought." *The Muslim World* 68 (1978): 259–284.

Conrad, Lawrence I. "The Conquest of Arwad: A Source-Critical Study in the Historiography of the Early Medieval Near East." *The Byzantine and Early Islamic Near East I: Problems in the Literary Source Material* Edited by Averil Cameron and Lawrence I. Conrad, 317–401. Princeton, NJ: the Darwin Press, 1992.

Crone, Patricia. *Medieval Islamic Political Thought*. The New Edinburgh Islamic Surveys. Edinburgh: Edinburgh University Press, 2006.

Dakake, Maria Massi. *Charismatic Community: Shi'ite Identity in Early Islam*. Albany, NY: State University of New York Press, 2007.

Donner, Fred M. *Muhammad and the Believers: At the Origins of Islam*. Cambridge, MA: Belknap Press of Harvard University Press, 2010.

_____. *Narratives of Islamic Origins: The Beginnings of Islamic Historical Writing*. Princeton, NJ: Darwin Press, 1998.

El-Hibri, Tayeb. *Parable and Politics in Early Islamic History: the Rashidun Caliphs*. New York, NY: Columbia University Press, 2010.

Fisher, Greg. *Between Empires: Arabs, Romans, and Sasanians in Late Antiquity*. Oxford: Oxford University Press, 2011.

Gershoni, Israel and James P. Jankowski. *Redefining the Egyptian Nation, 1930–1945*. New York, NY: Cambridge University Press, 1995.

Hinds, Martin. "Kufan Political Alignments and Their Background in the Mid-Seventh Century A.D." *International Journal of Middle East Studies* 2:4 (1971): 346–367.

_____. "The Murder of the Caliph 'Uthman." *The International Journal of Middle East Studies*. 3:4 (1972): 450–469.

Hourani, Albert. *Arabic Thought in the Liberal Age 1798–1939*. Cambridge, UK: Cambridge University Press, 1962.

Hoyland, Robert G. *In God's Path: The Arab Conquests and the Creation of an Islamic Empire*. New York, NY: Oxford University Press, 2015.

_____. *Seeing Islam as Others Saw it: A Survey and Evaluation of Christian, Jewish, and Zoroastrian Writings on Early Islam*. Princeton, NJ: Darwin Press, 1997.

Humphreys, R. Stephen. *Mu'awiya ibn Abi Sufyan: From Arabia to Empire*. Oxford: Oneworld Publications, 2006.

Husayn, Taha. *Al-Fitna al-kubra: 'Uthman ibn 'Affan*. Cairo: Dar al-ma'arif, n.d.

Kaegi, Walter E. *Byzantium and the Early Islamic Conquests*. Cambridge, UK: Cambridge University Press, 1995.

Keaney, Heather. *Medieval Islamic Historiography: Remembering Rebellion*. New York, NY: Routledge, 2013.

_____. "Taha Husayn, Tabari and the Future of History in Egypt," in James E. Lindsay and Jon Armajani, eds., *Historical Dimensions of Islam: Essays in Honor of R. Stephen Humphreys*. Princeton: Darwin Press, 2009.

Kennedy, Hugh. *The Great Arab Conquests: How the Spread of Islam Changed the World We Live In*. Philadelphia, PA: Da Capo, 2007.

Khalafallah, Hayfa. "'Abbas al-'Aqqad: The Historian." *The Arab Studies Journal* 3:1 (1995): 80–93.

Kohlberg, Etan, ed. *Shi'ism*. The Formation of the Classical Islamic World Series, edited by Lawrence Conrad Vol. 33. London: Routledge, 2003.

Pourshariati, Parvaneh, *Decline and Fall of the Sasanian Empire: The Sasanian-Parthian Confederacy and the Arab Conquest of Iran*. London: I.B. Tauris, 2008.

Reynolds, Gabriel Said, ed. *New Perspectives on the Qur'an: The Qur'an in its Historical Context 2*. London: Routledge, 2011.

_____. *The Qur'ān and Its Biblical Subtext*. London: Routledge, 2010.

_____ ed. *The Qur'an in its Historical Context*. London: Routledge, 2008.

Rippin, Andrew. "Literary Analysis of Qur'ān, Tafsir, and Sira: The Methodologies of John Wansbrough." *Approaches to Islam in Religious Studies*. Edited by Richard C. Martin, 151–163. Oxford: Oneworld Publications, 2001.

Robinson, Chase. *Islamic Historiography*. Cambridge, UK: Cambridge University Press, 2003.

Sizgorich, Thomas. "'Do Prophets Come with a Sword?' Conquest, Empire, and Historical Narrative in the Early Islamic World." *The American Historical Review* 112:4 (2007): 993–1015.

Smith, Charles, "The 'Crisis of Orientation': The Shift of Egyptian Intellectuals to Islamic Subjects in the 1930s." *International Journal of Middle East Studies* 4 (1973): 382–410.

Ṭabataba'i, Muhammad Husayn. *Shi'ite Islam*. 2nd edn. Persian Studies Series, No. 5. Translated by Seyyed Hossein Nasr. Albany, NY: State University of New York Press, 1977.

Vacca, Alison. *Non-Muslim Provinces under Early Islam: Islamic Rule and Iranian Legitimacy in Armenia and Caucasian Albania*. Cambridge, UK: Cambridge University Press, 2017.

Webb, Peter. *Imagining the Arabs: Arab Identity and the Rise of Islam*. Edinburgh: Edinburgh University Press, 2016.

Whelan, Estelle. "Forgotten Witness: Evidence for the Early Codification of the Qur'ān." *Journal of the American Oriental Society* 118:1 (1998): 1–14.

Yazigi, Maya. "Hadith al-'Ashara or the Political Uses of a Tradition." *Studia Islamica* 86 (1997): 159–167.

MEDIEVAL SOURCES

Al-Baldhuri, Ahmad b. Yahya. *Ansab al-ashraf* Vol. 4. Edited by Ihsan Abbas. Wiesbaden: Franz Steiner Verlag, 1979.

_____. *Kitab al-futuh al-buldan*. Translated by P. K. Hitti and Francis Murgotten as *The Origins of the Islamic State*, 2 vols. Columbia University Studies in History, Economics, and Public Law, Vol. 68, nos. 163, 163a. New York, NY: Columbia University Press, 1916–1924.

Ibn al-'Arabi, Abu Bakr. *Al-'Awasim min al-qawasim*. Edited by 'Ammar Halbi. Cairo: Maktabat Dar al-turath, 1997.

Ibn Bakr, Muhammad b. Yahya. *Al-Tamhid wa'l-bayan fi maqtal al-shahid 'Uthman b. 'Affan*. Edited by Mahmud Y. Zayid. Beirut: Dar al-Thaqafa, 1964.

Ibn Khaldun. *The Muqaddimah*. Translated by Franz Rosenthal; edited and abridged by N. J. Dawood, Bollingen Series. Princeton, NJ: Princeton University Press, 1969.

Ibn Sa'd, Muhammad. *Kitab al-tabaqat al-kabir*. Edited by Joseph Horovitz and Edward Sachan. Leiden: E.J. Brill, 1904.

Ibn Shabbah, Abu Zayd 'Umar. *Kitab ta'rikh al-madina al-munawwarah*. Edited by 'Ali Muhammad Dadhal and Yasin Sa'd al-Din Bayan. Beirut: Dar al-Kutub al-'Ilmiyyah, 1996.

Muhibb al-Din al-Tabari, Ahmad b. 'Abdallah. *Al-Riyad al-nadira fi manaqib al-'ashara*, 4 vols. Beirut: Dar al-Kutub al-'Ilmiyya, n.d.

Al-Tabari, Muhammad ibn Jarir. *The History of al-Tabari, Vol. XIV: The Conquest of Iran*. Translated by G. Rex Smith. Albany, NY: SUNY Press, 1994.

_____. *The History of al-Tabari, Vol. XV: The Crisis of the Early Caliphate*. Translated by R. Stephen Humphreys. Albany, NY: SUNY Press, 1990.

INDEX